▲ *The Battle of Pavia in 1525 was a crushing defeat for French King Francis I, when his knights were shot down by Spanish gunmen and his 28,000-strong army was annihilated. Yet he felt that because he had not disgraced himself, his honour survived.*

kept his honour safe, all other things could be lost. King Francis I of France famously declared after his humiliating defeat in the Battle of Pavia, northern Italy, in 1525, 'All is lost save honour'.

HOW R

There we knights did not live up to the code of chivalry that we are justified in asking to what extent they believed in it. Many institutions presented as noble expressions of chivalry had a very mundane side: for example, in one light, the 'brotherhood of arms' was little more than a very practical risk-sharing and profit-sharing arrangement, in which knights agreed to pay one another's ransoms and also to split any money they made. While the chronicles wrote up deeds of high chivalry, knights were indulging in pillage and looting, and often making great fortunes as a result. It could be argued that knights used chivalry as a smokescreen behind which they were happy to fight dirty wars.

Yet knights did often act in accordance with chivalry when dealing with one another – for example they went to great lengths and into personal danger to keep their honour. They saw knighthood as an international elite body, and it appears that they believed in the code of chivalry only as it applied to other members of the elite.

pressing vow. It depended upon honesty. In theory, honour reigned in both history and literature, as countless deeds were done because a knight had given his word of honour. For example, Sir Walter Manny led a contingent of just 50 knights in a highly dangerous attack on the French in 1339 because he had made a vow to be the first into combat in the war that had recently been declared (which became the epic Hundred Years War).

In reality, many a blind eye must have been turned to knights' actual behaviour. For instance, Sir John Talbot – one of the great English commanders in the Hundred Years War – was mourned at his death in 1453 as one of a dying breed of great knights, exemplars of chivalry, yet in his lifetime he was also known as a disturber of the peace and a ruthless operator.

Honour was all, the supreme concept of the chivalric code. Thus, if a knight

AFTER THE FALL

Medieval philosophers traced the origin of warfare and violence to the biblical Fall. According to the account in the Book of Genesis, our first ancestors Adam and Eve were expelled from the paradise of the Garden of Eden after they had defied God's commandment not to eat from the Tree of Knowledge in the garden. The Fall referred to this lapse from the original state of grace, living alongside God in the Garden, to the familiar conditions of life in the world. The medieval writers argued that war was the result of the Fall, and that God oversaw the rise of knights and the development of chivalry in order to regulate violence and defend those who were defenceless in the fallen world. Some authorities saw the origin of the knight in the Roman era, when they believed armed forces of 1,000 expert warriors were created.

▶ *Warfare followed the Fall and knights had to keep order and protect virtue.*

TALES OF WAR AND LOVE

HOW EPIC CHANSONS, ROMANCES AND COURTLY POEMS SHAPED CHIVALRY

By the *chansons de geste* and prose or poetry romances of chivalric literature, knights were educated in chivalry. As they listened to tales of great deeds, of battles won, tournaments fought, quests pursued or dread marvels encountered and overcome, they participated in the growing development of a vision of knighthood that would have a major influence on their own behaviour as knights.

THE MYTHS SURROUNDING KNIGHTHOOD

This vision embodied how knights should behave and how they should conduct themselves in an ideal world. These ideals often filtered through stories about how knights used to behave in a legendary or quasi-historical golden age of the past. Tales of Charlemagne and his paladins, of King Arthur and his knights, of biblical or classical warriors such as the Jewish freedom fighter Judas Maccabeus or the Macedonian conqueror Alexander the Great, were expositions of knightly virtue.

HEROIC DEEDS FROM A GOLDEN PAST

The first flowering of chivalric literature came in the 12th century, with the appearance of *chansons de geste* ('songs of heroic deeds'). These were epic poems in Old French that celebrated the exploits of Christian knights fighting for Charlemagne and other Frankish kings against warriors of Islam from Spain, usually called 'Saracens' (a word traditionally said to be derived from the Arabic *sharqiyin*, which meant 'easterners').

Some of the great deeds celebrated were based on historical fact – like those recounted in the first and greatest *chanson de geste*: the *Chanson de Roland* (*Song of Roland*) of *c*.1130–70, which as we have

▲ Minnesänger, *the German musician poets, were counterparts of the Provençal troubadours. Their songs included some written by kings and other leading nobles.*

seen was inspired by an ill-fated expedition to Spain led by Charlemagne in 778. The poems usually looked back to a lost golden age when knights behaved better, and so had an elegiac quality that is a strong part of their appeal.

The chansons were recited and sung by *jongleurs*, or minstrels, who would usually accompany themselves on a *vielle* – the medieval version of the violin. Chansons were probably composed and performed for around 200 years before the mid-12th century, the date of the oldest surviving manuscript. Around 100 chansons survive in manuscripts dating from the 12th to the 15th century.

◄ *The warlike feats and noble deeds of Charlemagne, seen here on the right, and his retainers, were the subject of many* chansons de geste, *most famously in the* Song of Roland, *illustrated here.*

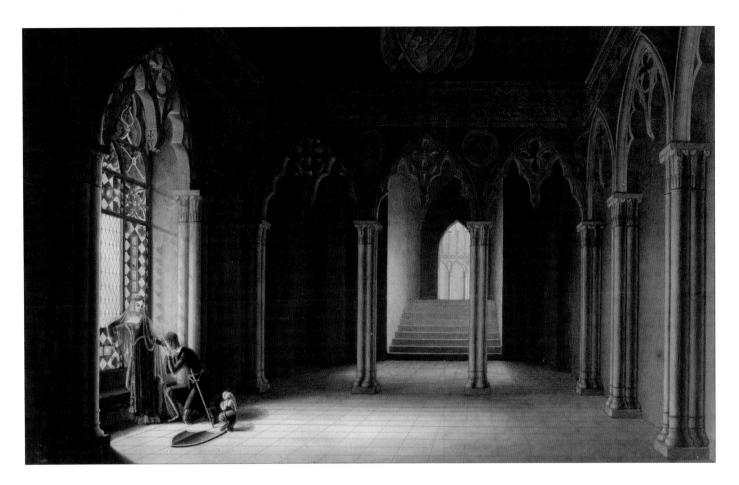

RISE OF ROMANCE

Alongside the *chansons de geste*, and ultimately superseding them, arose chivalric romances – narratives of heroic deeds written in prose or poetry. The romances flourished from the mid-12th century onwards throughout the age of chivalry – right up to the 16th and 17th centuries – but were at their most popular in *c.*1150–1300. According to the 12th-century Old-French poet Jean Bodel, there were three principal subjects for romances: 'the Matter of Rome', narratives about heroes of the classical world such as Julius Caesar; 'the Matter of France', principally stories about Charlemagne, his great knight Roland and other paladins; and 'the Matter of Britain', recounting the doings of King Arthur and the Knights of the Round Table. There was some common ground between chansons and the early romances. Both were written not in Latin, the language then used for scholarly and ecclesiastical writing, but in vernacular languages; the Old French word *romanz* means 'the language of the people'. A great

▲ *In the tradition of courtly love, knights were inspired to deeds of chivalry by their burning desire to prove themselves worthy of their lady's love.*

literary figure such as Chrétien de Troyes was the author of both romances and chansons, and they could have very similar subject matter. But one key difference was that chansons were performance poems that were sung to an audience by a professional troubadour, while romances were written down in a book and then read aloud.

COURTLY LOVE

In the late 11th century, in what is now southern France, poets developed a new emphasis in songs about knights. Working at the largely peaceful and prosperous courts of princes and dukes in Aquitaine, Burgundy, Champagne and Provence, the poets sang about knights' intense devotion to noble ladies. The knights conceived a fierce love for the ladies at court, who were often already married; the poets said

that the knights were bound to the ladies by the bonds of feudal service, as a knight conventionally was to his feudal lord.

This culture or literary convention has been known as one of 'courtly love' since the Frenchman Gaston Paris first used the term in the 19th century. It referred to the fact that the conventions flourished at royal and noble courts, and also to the supposed 'courts of love' at which, according to some of the poems, ladies sat in judgement on the exploits of their devoted admirers. Modern historians point out that the term 'courtly love' appeared only once in chivalric literature – in the form *cortez amor* in the 12th-century poem written by Pierre d'Alvernhe – and some writers prefer the name *fin'amors* ('fine love'), which was used frequently in poems of the period. It was an elevated form of love, characterized by the knight's feelings of devotion, almost to the point of religious worship, for the lady, and by humility and courtesy; it did have a sexual element, but actual physical consummation was not its principal goal.

NOBLE WARFARE

FIGHTING TO KEEP GOD'S PEACE

Knights believed that armed conflict was a quite proper way to settle disputes. It was honest and noble to confront an enemy in a trial of strength and martial skill. The chivalric attitude was that war is man's natural condition.

The 14th-century Provençal writer on chivalry, Honoré Bonet, declared in his *Arbre des Batailles* ('Tree of Battles') from 1382–87: 'Fighting is not a bad thing, but excellent and full of virtue, for it cannot be denied that war only seeks to put wrongs right, and turn disagreement to concord, in line with the teachings of Scripture'. Bonet's book, which is based on the *Tractatus de Bello* ('Theories of War') by the 14th-century Italian canon lawyer Giovanni da Legnano, argued not that all fighting was good, but that in the right context and for the right purpose, warfare was a noble and just cause. Churchmen and those who wrote on chivalric issues

▲ *A French manuscript illumination from c.1310–25 depicts the belief in those times that the crusaders were the knights of Christ in their campaign against Islam.*

generally agreed with this position, and argued that knights were ordained by God to keep order and peace while protecting and fighting in the Church's interests.

ATTEMPTS TO CONTROL PRIVATE WAR

There were often incidental victims when knights worked out their disagreements in 'private wars'. Peasants or churchmen might have livestock killed or lands ravaged in the fighting; they were not equipped to defend themselves against a lord and his well-armed warriors. From the 10th century onwards, the Church aimed to control rather than prevent the knights' outbursts of martial energy. Through the 'Peace of God' and the 'Truce of God' movements, churchmen tried to guarantee exemption from violence for certain groups such as peasants and clergy and attempted to outlaw fighting between knights on certain days – initially, Sundays and holy days and later the period of Lent.

Repeatedly kings, too, attempted to end the fighting of private wars, but with very limited success. The waging of private war remained a jealously guarded chivalric right – less in England, where knights did

not fight in this way after the 1200s, than in France and Germany. In France *c.*1350 the knight's right to wage war was reaffirmed by the French royal official, poet and legal expert Philippe de Beaumanoir, who wrote: 'A knight can wage war in line with tradition.' This entitlement was governed by certain rules: before attacking, a knight had to make a formal complaint against another, giving due cause, and the combatants were not permitted to burn or ravage property. In Germany private war also had a legal basis in the mid-14th century: Holy Roman Emperor Charles IV accepted the knight's entitlement to wage private war provided he gave his enemy three days' notice of attack.

PURSUING A QUARREL

Even when knights did not openly pursue private wars, there were many opportunities for them to settle grievances or seek out old opponents. When knights fought at tournaments, they had a good chance

▼ *In his youth Holy Roman Emperor Charles IV was wounded at Crécy; later he was known chiefly for his diplomatic skills and dedication to learning.*

▲ Medieval writers generally agreed that knights could justly wage war to keep the peace or protect the Church, but these battles could involve the knights in political maneouvrings – such as the campaigns to promote the interests of the papacy in Italy.

to come up once more against former adversaries. Private war could also be fought under cover of national war – many old quarrels were pursued during the Hundred Years War or the Scottish border raids on northern England.

Knights who fought private wars or who sought out former foes in this way were not merely pursuing a grudge, for often there was a strong chivalric element to the conflict: the knight who tracked down an old foe might not so much be seeking to get even as to pit himself once more against an honoured adversary in a 'joust of war' or a 'feat of arms'.

CHIVALRY IN COMBAT

In one of the most celebrated feats of arms, Scottish knight Sir David Lindsay of Glenesk fought Lord de Welles, England's ambassador to Scotland, on St George's Day 1390 on London Bridge in the presence of a great crowd and of King Richard II of England. Lord de Welles had boasted of English chivalry and so Sir David had challenged him to a test of strength, the rules of which called for a joust.

When the two knights met in the charge their lances both splintered, and onlookers taunted Sir David by calling out that he was tied to the saddle in contravention of the rules of conflict. To prove them wrong, the Scottish knight leapt from his horse then vaulted back into the saddle unaided before riding on.

At the second charge both lances again shattered; at the third joust, Sir David unseated Lord de Welles, who fell heavily

but recovered in time to fight on foot, when he was again defeated and this time quite badly injured. The Scots knight had Lord de Welles at his mercy but rather than press home his advantage, he revived his opponent – and after the contest visited him daily for three months during the lord's recuperation.

Sir David was widely praised for his gallantry – and chroniclers noted that he had fought in the true chivalric manner, not from anger but seeking glory. Later Sir David served as Scotland's ambassador to England, and he also commemorated his victory on St George's Day by founding a chantry at Dundee.

Three years afterwards, a second match between the leading lights of Scottish and English chivalry was held at London Bridge. On this occasion the English knights were the victors, in a conflict once again fought in the spirit of chivalry.

▼ How a knight fought was as important as why he did so – he was called upon to conduct himself bravely and to demonstrate that glory was more important to him than mere victory.

A KNIGHT FEARLESS AND BOLD

PIERRE DE TERRAIL, CHEVALIER DE BAYARD

French knight Pierre de Terrail achieved remarkable feats of chivalry while in the service of Kings Charles VIII, Louis XII and Francis I of France in the late 15th and early 16th centuries. In an age when chivalry appeared to be in severe decline, and when many knights were fighting as mercenaries for whoever paid the most, he was revered as a great example of the knightly creed and an unconditionally loyal servant of the French crown.

Pierre de Terrail was hailed as *le chevalier sans peur et sans reproche* ('the fearless and blameless knight'), and was the subject of a romanticizing biography by Jacques de Mailles.

▼ *The Chevalier de Bayard acted with typical gallantry in the siege of Brescia in 1512, when he was wounded, but his fellows in the victorious French army embarked upon a five-day sacking of the city, killing thousands.*

PIERRE DE TERRAIL

Born: 1473

Died: 30 April 1524

Knighted: 1495

Famous for: chivalrous bearing at all times

Greatest achievement: the defence of Mézières with a force of just 1,000 men against an army of 35,000

PAGE, SQUIRE AND KNIGHT

Born at Château Bayard in the Dauphiné, Pierre came from a great chivalric family, and in his youth served as page to Charles the Warrior, Duke of Savoy, before, at the age of 14, becoming a squire in the service of King Charles VIII of France. Even at a young age he was renowned for his handsome looks and his courteous and charming manners, as well as for his bravery and skill at jousting. He was a squire

in Charles's army at the start of the Italian Wars, launched by the French king against the kingdom of Naples, and fought in the Battle of Fornovo in 1495. The French lost the battle against a combined army from Venice, Milan and Mantua, but Terrail won glory when he captured an enemy standard, and afterwards he was knighted on the field of battle for his prowess. Subsequently Terrail was captured when pursuing an enemy, alone, into Milan, but he impressed and charmed his captor Ludovico Sforza, Duke of Milan, so much that the duke released the knight without demanding ransom.

HERO OF THE ITALIAN WARS

Terrail won repeated acclaim for his feats of bravery and chivalric deeds during the Italian Wars, on one occasion being the hero of a contest that took place between 12 French and 12 German knights, on another reputedly holding a bridge over

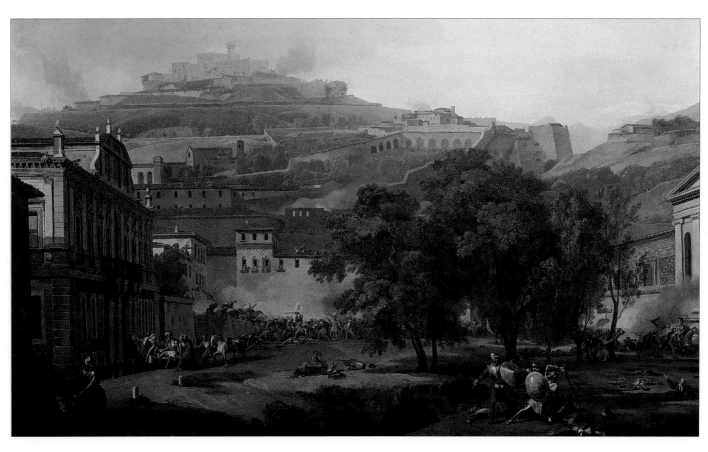

the river Garigliano in central Italy alone against a force of 200 Spanish knights. As in the chronicle accounts of Jean Froissart, the romantic nature of chivalry must have coloured the telling of his life story.

He was praised for his part in the sieges of Genoa in 1508 and of Padua in 1509 and was injured attempting to be the first on to the ramparts at the siege of Brescia in 1512. He was left unable to defend himself, but his soldiers took him to safety in the house of a nobleman; even severely wounded, he managed to do enough to prevent the nobleman's family from being insulted later in the siege. Then, before he was even properly recovered, he rode from Brescia to fight in the Battle of Ravenna under Gaston de Foix, Duke of Nemours.

In addition to bravery in combat, the Chevalier was known for his careful planning and sound knowledge of enemy movements gathered through painstaking reconnaissance and the use of spies.

▼ *A king kneels before a knight at Marignano, in 1515, when the Chevalier de Bayard knights young King Francis I.*

CAPTIVE OF KING HENRY VIII

The following year, in the wake of the French army's heavy defeat by King Henry VIII of England at the Battle of the Spurs, he attempted to rally the French but was isolated on the battlefield and, unwilling to surrender, he rode up to an English captain and demanded that he instead surrender; when the Englishman did so, the Chevalier de Bayard gave himself up. Henry VIII was delighted by the French knight's courtesy and chivalry and once again Terrail was released without ransom. He gave the English king his *parole*, or word of honour, that he would not fight in the war for a period of six weeks.

SAVIOUR OF FRANCE

In 1515 after playing a great part in the French victory in the battle of Marignano against a Swiss army in Italy, Terrail had the honour of knighting his own king, the 21-year-old Francis I. His biographer noted that despite the Chevalier's relative lack of social status, his bravery in battle meant that there was no one knight more worthy to raise the king to knighthood.

The Chevalier de Bayard was appointed Lieutenant-General of the Dauphiné and in 1521 defended the town of Mézières in northern France against the invading army of Holy Roman Emperor Charles V. For six weeks Terrail and his small garrison defied the imperial army, until eventually they lifted the siege. His actions prevented the invasion of central France and won time for Francis I to collect the army that would go on to defeat the imperial forces in 1521. He was hailed as France's saviour and made a knight of the Order of St Michael. He was given his own command of a unit of 100 mounted cavalry – an honour only previously given to scions of the royal family.

A CHIVALRIC DEATH IN ITALY

In Italy once more, in 1524, he took command of the French army after Admiral Guillaume de Bonnivet was wounded at Robecco. Terrail was himself fatally injured on 30 April when he was hit by a ball fired

▲ *Perhaps the Chevalier's finest achievement was inspiring a garrison of just 1,000 men to hold Mézières for six weeks against a 35,000-strong army of the Holy Roman Empire in 1521.*

from an arquebus (an early gun) during a skirmish at the crossing of the River Sesia. Like the English knight Sir John Talbot, he was killed by a gun, a fact that only reinforced the sense that here was one of the last of a dying breed of chivalric knights, representatives of an old and increasingly outmoded way of fighting. In Terrail's case, another important part of his appeal for contemporaries was that in addition to great prowess and spotless honour, he also showed kindness and had a light, carefree and charming manner. His second nickname was *le bon chevalier* ('the good knight').

The Chevalier died in the middle of battle, amidst his enemies, and attended by his old comrade in arms, Charles, Duke of Bourbon. Tradition has it that his dying words were as purely chivalric as his life: 'Do not pity me, for I died an honourable death while doing my duty. Pity rather those who fight against their king, their country or the sworn oath.'

BROTHERHOOD OF ARMS

A PARTNERSHIP BETWEEN KNIGHTS

The chivalric virtue of faithfulness was given powerful expression in the custom of the brotherhood of arms. Two knights pledged loyalty to one another, even to death.

BLOOD BROTHERS

Knights who swore to be brothers in arms took an oath to support one another in war and in peace: they would fight together, in some cases sharing the same coat of arms. Their vows meant that an enemy of one would be an enemy of the other, and likewise they would share friends and allies. The oath was stronger than any other tie that bound them except for the feudal duty to lord or king. It even took precedence over a knight's promises to his lady.

The custom probably had ancient roots that run back to the bonds of blood brotherhood made between Germanic and ancient Greek warriors who mixed their blood and swore to brave injury and death in defending one another. The medieval brotherhood of arms was usually formalized in a written document and to mark this contract the two men would take the Sacrament of Holy Communion as well as mixing their blood. They also exchanged a 'kiss of peace'.

KNIGHTS BOUND IN DEATH

The bond of Sir William Neville and Sir John Clanvowe epitomized the brotherhood of arms – although the written document giving evidence of their union unfortunately did not survive. The two men, both Knights of the Garter, died and were buried alongside one another in 1391 near Constantinople – and their tombstones are now exhibited in Istanbul's archaeological museum.

The stones depict the men's coats of arms combined, so that both bear the same shield showing the Neville and Clanvowe arms side by side – in heraldry

▲ *Chivalric encounters took place in the intervals between bouts of fighting during sieges and on campaign. Remarkably, even the tunnels excavated beneath castle walls to weaken the fortifications were large enough to be used for jousting.*

this is called 'impalement' and was customarily done to the arms of married couples. Sir William and Sir John were prominent knights who were constantly in each other's company from 1378 onwards, and their deaths were recorded in the chronicle of Westminster Abbey; we know from this source that when Sir John died, Sir William pined away – refusing to eat, weakening swiftly and dying himself just two days later. The chronicle refers to Sir William as Sir John's 'companion on the march'.

SHARING THE KISS OF PEACE

Many leading knights and princes were brothers in arms through the age of chivalry. As early as the 10th century, according to the chronicler Henry of Huntingdon, the kiss of peace was shared by Edmund Ironside and King Canute. In the 11th century Godfrey of Bouillon and the Prince of Edessa became brothers in arms. In the 14th century the great French warriors Bertrand du Guesclin and Olivier de Clisson made an agreement of this kind. They swore to guard one another as brothers, and to keep the other apprised of any impending threat. In the 15th century King Louis XI of France became brother in arms to Charles the Bold, Duke of Burgundy.

BROTHERS NO MORE

Although the agreement, like that made by a married couple, was 'till death', there is a notable example of a brotherhood in arms being cancelled. As Earl of Hereford, Henry Bolingbroke swore to be brother in arms with Louis, Duke of Orleans, but when Henry deposed King Richard II of England to become King Henry IV in 1399, Louis cancelled the treaty of brotherhood. The brothers became enemies as Louis challenged King Henry to meet him at any place in France for combat with 100 knights and squires in each company. Although he deposed his king, Henry was a great chivalric figure and was renowned as one of the foremost jousters and fighters at tournaments in his day.

PROFIT-SHARING AGREEMENT

Chivalry cast a glow over the real world. Its ideal forms often had a very practical side. The brotherhood in arms was an expression of faith and martial brotherhood, but among kings, princes and leading nobles it could be a very useful diplomatic tool, used to promote or cement alliances.

The brotherhood sometimes had strong elements of a business arrangement. As part of their brotherhood agreement, described above, the French knights Olivier de Clisson and Bertrand du Guesclin swore to share equally all the lands and ransoms gained in conflict. Similarly, two squires in the army of King Henry V, Nicolas Molyneux and John Winter, agreed detailed financial arrangements when they swore to become brothers in arms in the church of St Martin at Harfleur in 1421: for example, they were each pledged to find the first £1,000 if the other needed to be ransomed, and they agreed that any money they made while on campaigning should be despatched quickly to England to the safety of London banks.

In this context, the brotherhood is comparable to a profit-sharing agreement made by knights in tournaments. As we have seen, William Marshal and Roger de Gaugi, a knight in the household of his royal master Henry the Young King, made a substantial fortune competing in tournaments of 1177–79.

BROTHERS IN THE MINES

During the sieges of castles, when the attackers dug mines in an attempt to undermine the walls, the defenders would excavate countermines, thereby creating tunnels in which fighting took place. The conflict, strangely, usually took the form of formal jousting between knights on the opposing sides – and it was the custom for the knights who fought in this way to afterwards become brothers in arms. At Limoges in 1370 John of Gaunt, Duke of Lancaster, reputedly fought French knight Jean de Villemur in this way, and subsequently it appears that de Villemur was spared when the city was captured.

GODFATHER IN ARMS

The *Siete Partidas* (Seven-Part Code), a law code composed in the reign of King Alfonso X 'the Wise' of Castile (1252–84), described a relationship between knights that was comparable to the brotherhood of arms. The man who ungirded the sword of a new knight would thereafter stand as the knight's 'godfather in arms': the knight was forbidden to fight against his godfather in arms or in any way work to his detriment; he was expected to support his godfather in arms in any conflict unless it were against his feudal lord or one of the members of his own family. As well as formulating statutory codes, the Seven-Part Code also contained writings on philosophy and theology.

▼ *Alfonso, King of Spain – known also as 'the Learned' – set up a school of translators in Toledo, whose work accelerated the transmission of Arabic and ancient Greek learning into Europe.*

KING OF CHIVALRY

KING EDWARD III OF ENGLAND

King Edward III of England was an internationally renowned chivalric figure, celebrated as the foremost Christian warrior of the mid-14th century. He did a great deal to foster chivalry in England. As an inspirational general, he led his army to major military victories in France; he was father to the warrior-prince Edward the Black Prince; he presided over many tournaments and he founded the Order of the Garter, which was openly based upon the Round Table of King Arthur.

PROTECTOR OF THE REALM

In his youth Edward had a solid education in the practical skills of knighthood, and he learned to read and write Latin and to speak French and English. However, as a teenager he became a pawn in the power struggle between his father Edward II and his mother Queen Isabella, supported by

▼ *The surrender of the Burghers at Calais, 1347, to the English army. Six townsmen offered their lives to King Edward III if the besieged populace could be spared.*

> ### EDWARD III
> **Born**: 12 November 1312
> **Died**: 21 June 1377
> **Knighted**: 1 February 1327
> **Famous for**: embodiment of chivalry, a great general, co-founder of the Order of the Garter
> **Greatest achievement**: victory at Crécy (1346)

her lover Roger Mortimer. Isabella and Mortimer used him to depose Edward II and he became 'Protector of the Realm' at the age of 14. He was knighted by the Earl of Lancaster prior to his coronation on 1 February 1327.

EARLY HUMILIATION

Edward's first military campaign, against the Scots in 1327, was not a success and almost resulted in his capture by a raiding party led by Sir James Douglas; when the English prepared to retaliate, the Scots fled, reputedly making Edward weep tears

of frustration. England agreed a peace with the Scots that recognized Robert the Bruce as King Robert I, but the humiliation of the campaign and the treaty rankled with Edward for many years.

In 1330 Edward seized power in England, aged 18, when he launched a night raid on Nottingham Castle and surprised his mother and Mortimer in their bedchamber. He sent Mortimer to the Tower of London and exiled his mother at Castle Rising, Norfolk.

TOURNAMENTS

From the start Edward was an enthusiastic tourneyer, and used the tournaments he organized and attended as opportunities to consolidate relations with the leading knights. In 1330 he attended tournaments at Dartford, Stepney and Cheapside.

In 1331 he attended three days of jousts at Stepney: 26 defending knights and 26 challengers, all dressed in costumes bearing a motif of a golden arrow, rode through London to St Paul's and said prayers before jousting in the marketplace. For another three-day joust in the same year, at Cheapside in London, all the defenders were dressed as Tartar knights and were led through the streets by a lady in costume as a 'damsel'. The king's enthusiasm for tournaments and the store he set by them as opportunities to foster unity can be seen in the fact that for both these events, he ordered all able-bodied knights in the country to attend.

IN SCOTLAND

Edward soon built a military reputation for himself. In the war against the Scots in 1333, he won a resounding victory over Sir Archibald Douglas and a Scottish army at the Battle of Halidon Hill by using the new defensive tactics that combined dismounted knights with archers. Edward fought again in Scotland in 1334–35 and 1336, during which he achieved an act of high chivalry by rescuing Katherine, Countess of Atholl, from the besieged castle of Lochindorb in the Highlands, but thereafter his attention was largely taken up with wars against France.

CLAIM TO THE FRENCH THRONE

From the start of his reign Edward had been pressing his claim to the French throne. This followed the death without issue in 1328 of his uncle Charles IV of France. In 1340 Edward declared himself King of France, defeated a French fleet in the naval Battle of Sluys, and invaded France – with little success on land. His first major victory came in 1346 with the campaign in Normandy that saw him win the famous Battle of Crécy, achieved by using the same defensive tactics that he had used at Halidon Hill 13 years earlier.

The triumph of Crécy was followed by the surrender of besieged Calais in 1347, and the defeat of the Scots (in Edward's absence) near Durham, where the Scottish king, David II, was captured. At Calais, according to chroniclers, Edward held six

▼ *King Edward III released David II (right) from captivity in 1357. The Scots paid a ransom of 100,000 marks for their king.*

▲ *Edward laid claim to the French throne prior to the campaign that led to his famous victory in the naval battle of Sluys in 1340.*

leading citizens of Calais as hostages, and was preparing to put the men to death when Queen Philippa begged him to spare them. Ever the chivalrous knight, he acceded to the wishes of the lady and the citizens were spared. (Chroniclers made much of Queen Philippa's involvement, but she was not in fact at Calais.)

CHIVALRIC CELEBRATIONS

These military successes in France and Scotland were celebrated with a great series of chivalric events that were used as an opportunity to parade prisoners of war and to make a statement of the king's international power. In 1348 Edward hosted tournaments in various cities, and it was during a Windsor event that he began the brotherhood of the Order of the Garter. The founding knights were all veterans of Crécy and tourneying companions of the king and the Black Prince, and the two 'sides' of knights (one led by the king and one led by the Black Prince) may have

been based on tournament teams. The year 1356 brought further military triumphs, including victory at Poitiers in which the Black Prince led an 8,000-strong army to victory over 50,000 French, and captured King Jean II. This year may have been the high point of Edward's international standing. He was unable to translate his successes into lasting gains in France: in 1360 Jean was released for a ransom of 3 million gold crowns and Edward renounced the claim to the French throne. Over the next two decades the land in France that Edward held was gradually lost to a resurgent French military.

A CHIVALROUS KING

Edward's standing in Europe was built on his success as a warrior and his status as a chivalric figure. The chronicler Jean le Bel of Liège called him 'noble', and most contemporary accounts stressed his honourable behaviour – especially in his dealings with women. Stories of the Countess of Atholl's rescue and Edward's giving way to Queen Philippa's plea for the lives of the Calais hostages presented him as a model of chivalry.

ORDERS OF CHIVALRY

KNIGHTLY IDEALS AND THE LAY CHIVALRIC BROTHERHOODS

From a distance, the 14th century's lay chivalric brotherhoods, such as the English Order of the Garter and the Castilian Order of the Banda, appear to be a stirring embodiment of knightly romance. However, their creation as national organizations with oaths of loyalty to the king ran counter to the international ideals of religious chivalry that found expression both in the stateless class of knights mobilized to fight the crusades, and in the deeply religious brotherhoods like the Orders of the Templars and the Knights Hospitallers.

▼ *The establishment of the Order of the Garter was a celebration of Edward III's famous victory at the Battle of Crécy, as well as a statement of the power and nobility of English knighthood.*

KNIGHTS OF THE GARTER

The model for the secular brotherhoods was the Round Table of knights described in the romances of King Arthur. King Edward III initially emphasized the romance of his proposed brotherhood. He announced his intention to form it at a feast and tournament held at Windsor Castle in January 1344. He invited knights and their ladies from throughout the realm; and the king, his minstrels and no fewer than 200 squires and knights were decked out in fine tunics for the occasion. After a day of feasting and jousting, on the second morning of the festival Edward and Queen Philippa attended Mass, then the king solemnly swore upon the Bible that he would found a brotherhood of knights of similar type and standing to the one established by King Arthur. He said

▲ *Edward III confers the Order of the Garter on the Black Prince. The order's first meeting was at Windsor on 23 April 1349.*

the brotherhood would have 300 knights, and that they should meet at Whitsun – which was the traditional time for the assembly of knights in the Arthurian romances. He began the building of a hall to be the headquarters of the brotherhood: St George's Hall, Windsor.

However, when the Order of the Garter was finally established in 1348, it was at least as much a ploy in support of Edward's claim to the French throne as it was a tribute to the legendary chivalric feats of King Arthur and the knights of Camelot. The knights were each given a blue and yellow garter – in the colours of France – and their motto *Honi soit qui mal y pense* ('Shame come to him who thinks evil of it') was almost certainly a reference to the king's claim in France, a suggestion that only those who backed Edward in his designs on France could be his brothers in chivalry. The colourful account of the motto being the king's response to an embarrassment for his mistress (see box) was a later embellishment.

The Order had only 26 members instead of the proposed 300. They were King Edward and the Black Prince, with 12 knights each in their company. The knights selected by King Edward and the Black Prince were their brothers in arms, who had fought beside one another at the Battle of Crécy two years earlier and won honour in the lists at the king's many tournaments. The creation of the order was a celebration of the great victory at Crécy and a statement of the power of English knighthood. The statutes of the order established that Edward would call on the Knights of the Garter first when he was planning a war campaign or any other act of chivalry – France should beware.

ENDURING FAME OF THE ORDER OF THE GARTER

Other secular chivalric brotherhoods of the 14th century included, among others, the Order of St George (created in Hungary in 1325), the Order of the Sash (created in Castile in 1332), the Order of

▼ *French knights of the Order of the Star take their oath before its founder, John II of France, then celebrate at a banquet.*

▲ *Philip III the Good, Duke of Burgundy, wears the jewel-encrusted collar of his chivalric Order of the Golden Fleece.*

St Catherine (created in the Dauphiné in the 1330s) and the Order of the Star (created in France in 1352). None of these achieved the reputation or enduring glory of the Order of the Garter. The Order of the Star failed principally because it required its knights to swear that they would never retreat in battle, and according to one chronicler half of its member-knights were killed in one battle in Brittany in 1353. Another reason was that its founder, King John II, was very unpopular among the nobility of his country, after clashes with leading nobles earlier in his reign.

CHIVALRY AND DIPLOMACY

The Order of the Golden Fleece, created by Philip the Good, Duke of Burgundy, in 1430, was modelled on the Order of the Garter. Duke Philip's brotherhood initially had 24 members plus the king, but this number was raised to 30 in 1433 and 50 in 1516. Its badge was a piece of sheepskin hanging from a jewel-encrusted collar and its motto was *Pretium laborum non vile*

('The reward of labour is not cheap'). The order's statutes provided that all disputes among members would be settled by the order and that the king was required to take the advice of the knights before embarking on a war.

The original membership of the Order of the Garter included three French knights who had served the English cause in France. It became common practice for other secular brotherhoods, especially the Order of the Golden Fleece, to use offers of membership as a tool in diplomatic negotiations.

THE BLACK PRINCE
EDWARD OF WOODSTOCK, PRINCE OF WALES

Edward the Black Prince was a central figure of English knighthood in the mid-14th century. Eldest son of King Edward III of England, he was famed for his martial prowess: he 'won his spurs' aged 16 in the great victory at Crécy in 1346, was a founder member of the Order of the Garter and was celebrated as a conquering hero for his part in the Battle of Poitiers ten years later, when he captured the French king Jean II.

THE YOUNG KNIGHT
Son of a great devotee of chivalry, Edward was truly born to knighthood. He had his own suit of armour by the age of seven, and was already a friend of knights by the age of ten, in 1340, when he lost money at gambling to Sir John Chandos. At the age of 13 he went with his father on military campaigns abroad, and in 1346 he fought at Crécy, where he acquitted himself superbly in the vanguard of the army and became a hero of the English while little more than a boy.

At one point in the battle, he was knocked to his knees and was captured by the count of Hainault, but almost at once was freed by English knight Sir Richard Fitzsimon. One report suggests that King Edward, seeing his son under pressure, sent knights to his aid, but that when they arrived at the spot they found the prince and his companions leaning nonchalantly on their swords. (The account of the battle

▲ *The Black Prince is celebrated for his crushing victories over the French at Crécy and Poitiers. The French lost more nobles in these two battles than to the Black Death.*

in Froissart's *Chronicles*, which suggests that King Edward watched while the prince's section of the army came under powerful attack and refused to send help with the words 'Let the boy win his spurs', is believed to be a legend.)

After the battle, Edward paid a tribute to King John of Bohemia, a great chivalric figure who had been killed fighting on the French side. Prince Edward adopted King John's emblem, an ostrich feather, and motto *Ich Dien* ('I serve') as his own; at first the prince's badge showed a single feather but later versions had three feathers, and this has remained the emblem of the Prince of Wales to this day.

RETURN FROM POITIERS
At the Battle of Poitiers in 1356, Prince Edward captured the French king Jean II and afterwards, according to the account by Jean Froissart, behaved with great

chivalry – serving the king at table, and praising the sovereign's performance in battle, as having outdone that of all the great French knights. Afterwards Edward took Jean to Bordeaux, where they were delayed by three months of peace negotiations, and then by sea to Plymouth, where the party arrived in May 1357.

▼ *Victory at Poitiers was helped by great leadership from Edward and superb discipline among his troops.*

THE BLACK PRINCE

Born: 15 June 1330
Died: 8 June 1376
Knighted: 12 July 1346
Famous for: bravery in battle, co-founder of the Order of the Garter
Greatest achievement: victory at the Battle of Poitiers, 1356, and capture of the French king, Jean II

Edward made a magnificent triumphal entry into London later that month amid great pageantry: on the road, he was 'attacked' by 500 knights disguised as bandits in a mock ambush, and in London he was welcomed by the city guilds in streets decorated with armour and beside fountains running with wine. His reputation and chivalric prestige could get no higher.

PRINCE EDWARD AND CHIVALRY

In many ways, Edward was an exemplar of chivalry. In addition to his treatment of Jean II, he was a great jouster and was noted for his generosity, his willingness to exhibit the knightly virtue of *largesse*. After Poitiers he rewarded his leading knights Sir James Audley and Sir John Chandos with gifts of 600 crowns, in addition to large annuities. He was also known for his piety – he made pilgrimages before campaigns (to Walsingham and Canterbury in 1345 and again to Walsingham in 1354), and made a number of generous donations to Canterbury Cathedral. He is believed to have been devoted to the Holy Trinity and is represented in a lead badge doing religious homage.

Prince Edward was surely destined to be one of England's greatest kings, but the length of his father's 50-year reign (1327–77) and the prince's own death in

▲ After being captured at Poitiers by Prince Edward, John II of France was escorted in style to captivity in England. He was valued at no less than 3 million crowns by his English ransomers.

his mid-40s from dysentery denied him that honour. In his time he was England's most famous knight. His use of some unchivalric methods, such as chevauchée raiding, was common in his time.

NAMED FOR HIS ARMOUR

In his lifetime the prince was called 'Edward of Woodstock' after his place of birth. The name of 'the Black Prince' was first used in an English chronicle that was

published by the Tudor printer Richard Grafton. Modern historians suggest that the name may have been made up by French chroniclers, and referred to his string of victories over the French or the cruelty of the chevauchée raiding he planned. The traditional view, however, is that the name was used because of an ornate black cuirass, or breastplate, given to the young prince by his father at the Battle of Crécy.

▼ A gilt-copper effigy of the Black Prince surmounts the knight's tomb in Canterbury Cathedral. Above the tomb is a panel of the Holy Trinity, to which Edward dedicated his chivalric achievements.

KNIGHTLY HEROES OF THE BIBLICAL AND CLASSICAL WORLDS

In his *Historia Regum Britanniae* (*History of the Kings of Britain*), written in *c.*1135–39, the chronicler Geoffrey of Monmouth claimed that the people of Britain were descended from Brutus, great-grandson of Aeneas of Troy. Geoffrey wrote that Brutus and his fellow Trojan Corineus were the first settlers of the British Isles: Brutus founded the city of Troia Nova ('New Troy'), which became London, while Corineus gave his name to Cornwall. Britain was thereby linked to the heroic past of legend, and perhaps also to the Roman Empire, which according to some was founded by Aeneas.

In the same way the strand of knightly poems and romances centred on classical heroes and biblical warriors added glory to contemporary knights by creating an ancient pedigree. Romance authors described the classical and biblical warriors as if they were medieval knights. Characters in the stories were intended to inspire knights to perform similar acts of chivalry.

For the purposes of this book, great figures such as the Jewish King David or the Greek warrior Achilles are of interest not in their own right as warriors, although their reputation makes them major figures in military history, but because the way they were presented in chivalric literature gives us important insights into how medieval authors and knights understood chivalry and their own world.

▲ *Medieval-style Trojans setting off for battle in a 15th-century manuscript.*

◀ *In the 15th century Alexander the Great was depicted riding into battle against the Persians in the manner of a late medieval king, with 12th-century armour and weapons.*

GOD'S SOLDIERS

AN INSPIRATION TO CRUSADERS

Knights of the Middle Ages saw the Jewish warriors of the Old Testament as exemplars of chivalry. Chief among these biblical prototypes of the medieval knight were King David, Judas Maccabeus, Joshua and Gideon.

THE CITY OF DAVID

In the 10th century BC David became the second king of Israel (after Saul) and created a united kingdom with a capital at Jerusalem (later called 'the city of David'). David was a great warrior as well as a king. The most famous of the many celebrated biblical stories featuring him was doubtless his slaying of the Philistine giant Goliath in single combat, using a stone from his sling. In the medieval Christian tradition he was likened to Christ himself, and his victory over Goliath was said to be the precursor of Christ's victory over evil in the form of Satan.

David was also a poet and musician – and is traditionally believed to be the author of much of the Book of Psalms in the Bible. He was one of the prototypes for those ideal chivalric figures and historical knights – such as King Richard I – who wrote poetry and songs as well as being great warriors.

THE HAMMER

Judas Maccabeus was a Jewish guerrilla fighter of the 2nd century BC, who led a revolt against the Seleucid empire, the Hellenistic state stretching from Thrace to India that followed Alexander the Great's empire. The Seleucid King Antiochus IV Epiphanes had attempted to prevent the Jews from practising their religion, had defaced the Temple in Jerusalem and rededicated it to the Greek god Zeus. Judas's rebellion against the Seleucids was celebrated for having saved Judaism.

Using mainly guerrilla tactics, Judas defeated four Seleucid armies and restored the Temple in Jerusalem. The name Maccabeus was given to him in his lifetime, and is thought to derive from the Aramaic word *maqqaba* ('hammer') – a reference to his fierceness in battle. In later years both Frankish king Charles Martel (Charles 'the Hammer') and English monarch Edward I (known as *Scottorum Malleus* – 'the Hammer of the Scots' – because of his victories in Scotland) were similarly honoured.

Judas's achievements were described in Books 1 and 2 Maccabees, which were part of the Bible in the medieval period. (The books are still part of the Old Testament in the Roman Catholic and Eastern Orthodox Christian traditions, but not in the Hebrew Bible. Protestant Christians usually consider them to be part of the Apochrypha, a group of texts associated with the Bible but not included in it.) Judas featured also in the history written by the 1st-century AD Jewish priest and historian Josephus.

AN EXAMPLE FOR CRUSADERS

Judas Maccabeus was celebrated for his strength, bravery and piety, and the combination of these qualities made him the ideal model for knights. In defending his faith of Judaism (seen as the forerunner of Christianity) and driving imposters

◄ *An illustration to 16th-century French manuscript shows the Jewish warrior Judas Maccabeus giving money to pay for services for those killed in battle.*

◄ The Israelites commanded by Joshua sack the city of Ai (top), and (below) the people of Gibeon, afraid of the receiving the same treatment, make peace with Joshua. Both images are from a 13th-century manuscript of the Old Testament.

Sadly, in victory the crusaders also followed the example of Joshua's army, when his men slaughtered every living person in Jericho except for a woman, Rahab, and her family who had helped spies sent ahead by Joshua before the attack. Once in Jerusalem, the crusaders likewise went on a violent rampage, until the streets ran with blood. (Joshua's exploits were described in the Bible, chiefly in the books of Exodus, Numbers and Joshua.)

Another great biblical warrior, Gideon, was hailed by medieval writers for his combination of martial power and deep religious faith. As described in the Bible's Book of Judges, he restored the true faith in God after his fellow Jews had turned to the worship of the Canaanite god Baal. Gideon won a great victory over a tribe of desert raiders called the Midianites. His name meant 'Great Warrior'.

out of the holy city of Jerusalem, he was a prototype for the knights of the crusades.

The example of the biblical warrior Joshua was also a model for the crusader knights, particularly those on the First Crusade. After the Israelites had escaped from captivity in Egypt in c.1200BC, Joshua succeeded Moses as their leader and led them into the 'Promised Land' of Canaan (the eastern Mediterranean shore, from southern Turkey to Egypt).

On arrival in Canaan, Joshua famously inspired the Israelites to attempt to capture the fortified city of Jericho. This was done by ordering the army to march around the city for seven days – after which the walls miraculously collapsed. In 1099 the priest Peter Desiderius convinced the crusaders to employ the same tactics at Jerusalem – and reputedly they were again successful.

THE NINE WORTHIES

Joshua, David, and Judas Maccabeus were celebrated as the three great exemplars of chivalry of the biblical age in the list of the Nine Worthies accepted by medieval writers. The idea of the Nine Worthies was introduced in a *chanson de geste* called *Les Voeux du Paon* ('A Peacock's Vows'), written in 1312 for the Bishop of Liège; the poem was traditionally said to have been written by Jacques de Longuyon from Lorraine, but this claim has been shown to be false. The list of the Nine Worthies also includes figures from the classical world – Hector of Troy, Alexander the Great and Julius Caesar; and the Christian era – King Arthur, Charlemagne, and crusader knight Godfrey of Bouillon.

▲ The warrior Judas Maccabeus, portrayed as one of the Nine Worthies.

HEROES OF ANCIENT GREECE
ANCIENT WARRIORS PRESENTED AS FEUDAL KNIGHTS

The 12th-century trouvère Benoit de Sainte-Maure gave the classical story of the Trojan War a feudal setting in his poem *Le Roman de Troie* (*The Romance of Troy*). In Benoit's 40,000-line poem, written in *c.*1160, all the Greek and Roman heroes of the narrative behaved as feudal warriors. They had abbeys and castles, and they fought according to 12th-century techniques of war.

The story of the Trojan War, which describes historical events that occurred in Anatolia in the 13th century BC, is principally familiar to modern audiences through the *Iliad,* by the ancient Greek poet Homer. However, Benoit de Sainte-Maure did not have access to the works of Homer, since these were not rediscovered until the 15th century in Italy. He had two main sources: a Latin history believed in the Middle Ages to have been written by Dares the Phrygian, a participant in the events described, which in fact probably dated from the 5th century AD; and another Latin account, supposedly written by a second contemporary, Dictys of Crete, but in fact dating from the 4th century AD.

Benoit's version was strikingly different from the accounts familiar to modern readers because it did not include the frequent interventions in the story by Greek gods and goddesses. It made the Trojan warrior Hector, rather than the Greek warrior Achilles, the main hero of

the narrative. This was in line with the prevailing enthusiasm for Troy and its heroes – Hector was celebrated, as we have seen, as one of three principal warriors and chivalric figures of the classical age in the list of Nine Worthies.

THE *ROMANS D'ANTIQUITÉ*
Benoit's poem inspired an entire literary genre, the *romans d'antiquité*, which consisted of poems of the feudal age featuring classical warriors – the 'Matter of Rome' described by Jean Bodel. Of these ancient warriors, the Greek Achilles and the Trojan

▲ *Hector leads the mounted warriors of Troy into the kind of battle fought by knights in the 15th century, when this edition of Benoit's Trojan poem was published.*

Hector were viewed as the finest exemplars of chivalry. The poems were intended to inspire contemporary warriors in the audience by their examples of great chivalric behaviour. The poets who wrote them invented love affairs for their protagonists so they could treat themes of courtly love, and added episodes of knight-errantry and fighting of tournaments so they could describe acts of gallantry and chivalry. Classical narratives of this kind were, alongside Arthurian stories, the favourite subjects for enactment in tournaments and the courtly pageants that surrounded them.

Benoit was attached to the court of King Henry II of England and dedicated *Le Roman de Troie* to Henry's queen, the

◄ *An illustration from an edition of Benoit de Sainte-Maure's* Romance of Troy *shows the Trojans building their city.*

▲ *This portrait of Hector of Troy is from a fresco of the Nine Worthies made in c.1430.*

great royal patroness of chivalric literature, Eleanor of Aquitaine. He may also have been the author of a slightly earlier romance called *Le Roman de Thèbes* (*The Romance of Thebes*), a 10,000-line account of the assaults by the city of Argos on the city of Thebes. It was based on an abridgement of the Latin poem the *Thebaid*, written in the 1st century AD by Publius Papinius Statius, and again represented the Greeks using 12th-century methods of warfare and behaving according to the dictates of courtly love.

Another near-contemporary poem is the 2,000-verse *Le Roman d'Eneas* (*The Romance of Aeneas*), again sometimes attributed to Benoit. Written in *c*.1160, it was presented as a translation of the Latin poem the *Aeneid* (written in the 1st century BC by Roman poet Virgil). However, rather than reproducing Virgil's account of the travels of Trojan warrior Aeneas from Troy to Italy and his defeat of the Latin people there, it instead concentrated on a medieval courtly love affair between Aeneas and Lavinia, daughter of Latinus, King of the Latins.

TROILUS AND CRESSIDA

Benoit's *Le Roman de Troie* imported the concerns of 12th-century courtly love into the world of the Greek war against Troy. He invented a love affair between a Trojan prince and Briseida, the daughter of a Trojan priest, and this was the first telling of the story of Troilus and Cressida, which was later retold by three major writers.

In Homer's narrative (which, as we have seen, was not available to Benoit) Troilus was the son of King Priam and Queen Hecuba of Troy, and was killed before the Trojan War began. In other ancient versions Troilus was killed by the Greek hero Achilles. In Benoit's poem, Troilus was presented as a young and innocent warrior, who fell deeply in love with the beautiful Briseida, but was betrayed by her when she took up with the Greek warrior Diomedes. The heroine was renamed Cressida in the three later accounts of the tale: the 14th-century version *Il Filostrato* (*c*.1335) by the Italian poet Giovanni Boccaccio; Englishman Geoffrey Chaucer took Boccaccio's work as the outline for his poem *Troilus and Criseyde*, written *c*.1385–90; and then, in the 17th century, William Shakespeare used Chaucer's poem as the source for his play *Troilus and Cressida* (*c*.1602).

In Boccaccio's poem, Cressida mourned for her father, Calcas, who had powers of prophecy and had seen the future defeat of Troy and so taken up residence in the Greek camp. Troilus noticed her at a festival and fell passionately in love with her. With the help of his friend Pandarus, a cousin of Cressida, he was able to meet her. As part of a truce agreement Cressida was then allowed to join her father in the camp, leaving Troilus in the city. He begged her to elope with him, but she said he should remain to defend Troy. She promised to guard her honour closely and meet him again after ten days.

Subsequently, however, Cressida was seduced by the Greek warrior Diomedes and she did not keep her promise to return to Troilus. He suspected the worst, and although Cressida sent him letters promising continuing love his fears were confirmed when his brother Deiphobus returned from battle with a piece of Diomedes' clothing – it had a favour from Cressida attached to it. Troilus sought revenge in battle, and fought for many hours against Diomedes, and in the style of a hero of chivalric romance killed no fewer than a thousand warriors in his righteous anger, but did not kill his rival. He was finally despatched by Achilles.

▼ *The go-between Pandarus talks to Cressida on behalf of her courtly lover Troilus. This image is from an edition of Giovanni Boccaccio's poem* Il Filostrato, *printed c.1475.*

THE ADVENTURES OF ALEXANDER
MEDIEVAL ROMANCES ABOUT ALEXANDER THE GREAT

A series of medieval romances recounted the larger-than-life exploits of Alexander the Great, the 4th-century BC Macedonian warrior who conquered the Persian Empire and northern India. The Alexander romances – like the *romans d'antiquités* that featured narratives of the heroes of Greece and Troy – used an anachronistic approach, presenting the great general and other ancient heroes as feudal warriors. They were also full of marvels and enchantments, monsters and magic, and tales of the Orient that appealed strongly to a noble audience that had developed a taste for the exoticism of the East, by listening to the eye-witness accounts of grizzled crusaders.

Alexander's extraordinary career combined stirring military achievements with explorations far into the east, beyond the limits of the known world. Even in his lifetime, colourful legends collected around his name and following his death in 323BC, a folklore rich in exotic oriental marvels grew up. A number of these stories, written in Greek, were gathered in

c. AD300 by an author masquerading as one of Alexander's own generals named Callisthenes, and the scholars call the text the pseudo-Callisthenes; many translations of this source in Latin were available to the authors of the romances in the 12th and 13th centuries.

ALBERIC OF BESANÇON
The oldest surviving medieval version of the life of Alexander was written in *c.*1100–1150 by Alberic of Besançon. Alberic told how Alexander's birth was

▲ *According to legend, the great warrior had a remarkable education. A French edition of* The Alexander Romance, *c.1400, shows him with his tutor Aristotle.*

marked by marvels: the sky grew dark as the sea raged and the rain fell red as blood, but with the birth of the baby who was destined to be a conqueror all fell quiet. According to the legend recounted by Alberic, Alexander's father King Philip II of Macedon appointed great men of the age of antiquity including Homer, Aristotle and Ptolemy to be tutors to Alexander in his youth; and they saw to it that he had a good chivalric education, of the kind enjoyed by the nobles in the audience for the poem, combining knowledge of letters with training in the arts of knighthood such as swordplay, jousting and hunting – as well as singing and playing music.

THE ALEXANDER ROMANCE
Alberic's work survives only in a fragment of 105 lines, but it was one of the major sources for other medieval stories about the legendary general, notably *Le Roman d'Alexandre* (*The Alexander Romance*), a

◄ *The people of Babylon give the keys of their city to Alexander. The world-conquering general died in Babylon, perhaps of food or alcohol poisoning, aged 33 in June 323BC.*

poem in lines of 12 syllables written by the Norman poet Alexander of Bernay, also known as Alexander of Paris, before 1200. (The 12-syllable lines he used to such good effect were named 'alexandrines' in his honour.)

EXTRAORDINARY FEATS

One section of *The Alexander Romance* told how as a youth the future general prefigured his wide conquests on land by claiming the heavens as his own. It happened that one day as he rode to hunt he saw two gryphons, creatures of Greek myth that combined a lion's body with an eagle's head and wings. He was seized by a desire to fly the creatures as high as the sun, and called a squire to him, commanding the young man to capture and starve the gryphons for two days, so that on the third day they would be willing to obey his commands if he brought them food. Meanwhile he constructed a chair and added a canopy to guard against the light when he was near the sun.

When the day came, he easily mastered the gryphons, tied the chair to them, and by luring them with juicy meat suspended just out of their reach he drove them into the sky as easily as he was able to make his horse gallop and turn in the hunt. He flew so high that the gryphons' wings were burned and the creatures swooped down away from the great heat; Alexander mastered them once more and brought them safely to land in his father Philip's fields.

Another episode recalls how he went on campaign to the land of the Amazons, the race of terrifying female warriors in Greek mythology, and forced them to pay tribute. Their queen, Thalestris, was so impressed with the general that she came to him with 300 women hoping to breed children in his image – she herself waited on him for 13 days and nights, in hopes that she might conceive a daughter by him.

THE WISDOM OF INDIA

Two other tales recounted incidents that occurred during Alexander's campaigns in India. In the first, Alexander encountered

a group of Indian sages, who informed him that they were not afraid of him because in their village there was nothing to steal except wisdom – and for all his strength, he could not take that from them against their will. In the story, Alexander reacted with grace and intelligence, allowing his army to rest in a camp and sitting with the sages in order to learn from them. They told him that all his campaigning would in the end be for nothing since he, like all men and women, would die, and another man would come and take what he had worked so hard to conquer; but they also taught him that death was not the end, for although darkness covered the soul when a person died, soon the soul would rise to new life just as the sun rose at the end of night.

▲ *After being impressed by war elephants in the Persian army during his victory at the Battle of Gaugamela in 331BC, Alexander incorporated the animals into his own forces and used them in battle charges.*

In the second story, which was framed as a letter from Alexander to his tutor Aristotle, the great general encountered in India a holy grove containing talking trees that were sacred to the moon and sun gods. The trees delivered the chilling news that Alexander would be killed by his own men and that his death would come in Babylon – a prophecy that proved only half-right, for although Alexander did die in Babylon in 323BC at just 33 years of age, it was from fever rather than as a result of treachery.

KNIGHT OF ROME

JULIUS CAESAR

Another great general of the classical world revered as an embodiment of chivalry was Julius Caesar, the Roman general and statesman, conqueror of France (then known as Gaul) in 58–50BC and invader of Britain in 55BC and 54BC.

ALL FOR LOVE

As we have seen, Caesar was one of the Nine Worthies who were presented as exemplars of chivalry. In the 14th-century French romance *Perceforest* (c.1330–44), he was portrayed as a young knight in the courtly love tradition, who decided to invade Britain because one of his own knights named Luces had fallen passionately in love with the wife of Perceforest, King of England.

The seeds of Caesar's death were sown in the invasion: after Caesar killed a British knight with a lance, the knight's nephew Orsus Bouchesuave vowed revenge, and taking the lance, made 12 iron weapons from its head. These were the weapons used by Brutus and his allies (with Orsus in their number) to kill Caesar on the Ides of March in 44BC.

The romance also found room for Alexander the Great: it claimed that he conquered Britain, but then set out for Babylon and left Perceforest in charge;

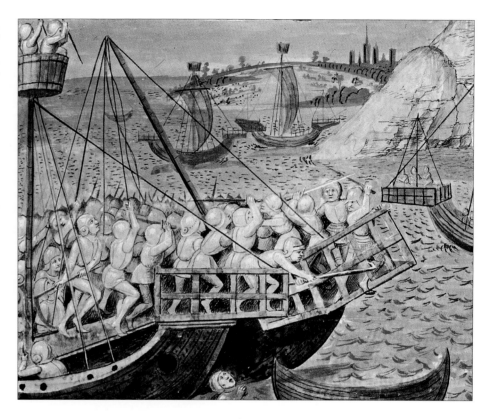

Perceforest then converted Britain to Christianity and ruled over a golden age, with bands of great knights in his service.

GEOFFREY OF MONMOUTH'S 'HISTORY' OF CAESAR

Geoffrey of Monmouth included an account of the Roman general's invasions of Britain in his *History of the Kings of*

▲ *A 15th-century French manuscript of the* Deeds of the Romans *depicts Caesar's army in full medieval armour preparing to disembark after defeating a Breton army.*

Britain (c.1135–39). To the various existing accounts by early medieval writers such as Bede and Nennius, Geoffrey added a number of legendary elements that reflected the preoccupations of the medieval knights in his audience.

According to Geoffrey's account, Julius Caesar decided to invade Britain after he had conquered Gaul (whereas in reality he undertook the invasions while still engaged in the conquest of Gaul) and dispatched a letter demanding tribute to Cassibelaunus, the King of Britain. (Cassibelaunus was Geoffrey's literary version of the historical British chieftain

◄ *The Roman army uses medieval siege engines and ladders to break into a fortress in this illustration from a 14th-century French edition of the* Deeds of the Romans.

Cassivellaunus of the Catuvellauni tribe, who led British resistance to the second Caesarian invasion that occurred in 54BC.) Cassibelaunus refused to pay tribute and claimed equality with Caesar, on account of the Romans' and Britons' common descent from the heroes of Troy.

CAESAR'S MAGICAL SWORD

Caesar then invaded via the Thames estuary and during the ensuing battle engaged in a hand-to-hand duel with Nennius, Cassibelaunus's brother. In the course of the struggle, Caesar struck Nennius a brutal blow to the head and then his sword *Crocea Mors* ('Yellow Death') became stuck in Nennius's shield. Nennius kept the weapon and – like the swords carried by great chivalric figures such as Charlemagne or King Arthur – it proved to be a sword of magical power that laid low any person that Nennius encountered during the remainder of the battle. The Britons fought with such heroism that Caesar was forced to take flight and sailed back to France. Nennius, however, survived for only 15 days after the battle and died from the effects of the head wound. He was buried in Trinovantum (London) with the magical sword beside him.

BRITONS BETRAYED

Subsequently, according to Geoffrey, Caesar invaded a second time and was driven back once more. The British used the cunning tactic of driving stakes into the Thames mud so they were hidden beneath the water at high tide and holed the Roman ships. During the victory celebrations after this triumph, however, the seeds of future disaster were sown when Cassibelaunus's nephew Hirelglas was killed by Cuelinus, the nephew of another royal, Androgeus, during a bout of wrestling. In Caesar's third invasion, Androgeus betrayed Cassibelaunus by

▲ *Caesar's assassination on the Ides of March 44BC is reimagined as a moment of 15th-century Italian court life in this panel of c.1450 by Giovanni di Tommaso Angelo.*

launching an attack on the rear of the British, and driving Cassibelaunus into retreat. Finally Cassibelaunus agreed to pay tribute to Caesar and became his friend.

AN ISLAND FOR A HORSE

Caesar and the invasion were also covered in the *Welsh Triads of the Islands of Britain*, a 13th-century collection of history, mythology and folklore. In this version, Cassibelaunus (here called Caswallawn) travelled to Rome to find his lover Fflur and initially allowed Caesar to land in Britain, in return for a horse of great strength and beauty named Meinlas.

ANCIENT VERSUS MEDIEVAL

Also in the 13th century a French work, *Le Faits des Romains* (*Deeds of the Romans*) detailed Caesar's invasion of Britain. In this the invaders overcame the underwater stakes by burning them with Greek fire. The mysterious Greek fire was a sulphur-based weapon developed in c.AD670 and used by the Byzantine Greeks. The use of the stakes was a partial invention of the medieval writers: in the historic invasion, the Britons did use sharpened stakes and did conceal some beneath the waterline, but they intended them as a defence against Roman infantry, not the ships.

ONE OF THE NINE WORTHIES

As with all the Nine Worthies, Julius Caesar (depicted below second left in an early 15th-century fresco) represents all facets of the perfect warrior. All, with the exception of Hector of Troy and arguably King Arthur, are conquering heroes. Most came from royal families.

All brought glory and honour to their nations and were noted for their prowess in arms. As individuals, each displayed some outstanding chivalric quality which, in combination with their historical context, made them exemplars of knighthood.

SIR ORFEO

CHIVALRIC LORD, LOYAL HUSBAND AND COURTLY MUSICIAN

An English poem from the 13th and 14th centuries transposed the Greek myth of Orpheus and Eurydice to the world of medieval England. The hero and heroine, in the Greek myth a minstrel and his beloved wife, a tree-spirit, became Sir Orfeo, ruler of a medieval kingdom, and his queen, Heurodis. The poem *Sir Orfeo* appeared to be derived from an earlier Old French Breton lay or song and it showed the strong influence of Celtic folktales about faery kingdoms existing alongside the day-to-day world.

WHAT MEDIEVAL POETS KNEW OF THE GREEK MYTH

The earliest surviving manuscript of *Sir Orfeo* dates from *c.*1330. There are references to a Breton lay about Orpheus in earlier French narratives, such as the 12th-century romance *Floire et Blanchefleur* (*Floris and Blanchefleur*) and the 13th-century *Prose Lancelot*, but this version of the story has not survived. The ancient Greek myth of Orpheus and Eurydice

▼ *According to the ancient Greek myth, Orpheus was killed by Maenads, female worshippers of the mystery god Dionysius. They were angry that after Eurydice's death he had abandoned the love of women.*

dates back to at least the 6th century BC, and would have been available to the medieval period poets through the Roman poets Virgil and Ovid.

In the Greek myth Orpheus was a musician from Thrace so gifted that animals, and even trees and stones, would come to listen to his playing of the lyre. When his wife Eurydice was killed by a snakebite he followed her into the underworld, and there played so beautifully that the god of the dead, Hades, allowed him to have Eurydice back – on the condition that as he led her out of the land of the dead, back to the world of the living, he did not look back. In older versions of the myth he succeeded, and Eurydice was restored to life, but in the better known, and less happy versions (found in Ovid and Virgil) he looked back – and Eurydice dissolved into mist.

FROM WINCHESTER TO THE OTHERWORLD

The poet of *Sir Orfeo* began by situating the narrative in England, declaring that Thrace (Orfeo's kingdom) was in fact an old title for Winchester, King Alfred the Great's capital. The king lost his beloved wife, Heurodis, when she was stolen by the king of the fairies from under an apple tree haunted by spirits. In this version, she did not die, but was taken at the moment before death to a faery Otherworld.

Sir Orfeo was undone by grief, and renounced his kingdom in order to search for Heurodis. Like a good feudal lord he thought of the well-being of his vassals, and left his steward in charge of the kingdom; he announced that the people should hold an assembly to elect a new ruler if they heard reports of his death. Then he cast off his fine clothes and put on the simple robes of a pilgrim, and retreated into the forest. He took only one thing with him: his harp. In his solitude and grief, deep in the woods, he played

▲ *Orpheus and Eurydice in elaborate medieval courtly dress, from an illustration to a c.1412 edition of the works of Venetian female writer Christine de Pizan.*

songs of unearthly beauty on this instrument, and even the wild animals were charmed to stillness.

Ten years passed, then one day Sir Orfeo saw Heurodis riding by in the fairy king's hunting expedition, and followed her into the Otherworld. There he played songs of exquisite beauty on his harp and the king offered him one 'boon', or favour. Seizing his chance, Sir Orfeo chose Heurodis and led her back to the earth.

With Heurodis safely restored to him, Sir Orfeo returned, rejoicing, to Winchester. He remained disguised as a poor beggar in order to test the loyalty of his steward, and finding the man to be honest and true, he then revealed his identity and resumed his rule as king.

▶ *The myth of Orpheus, with the journey to the underworld realm of the dead and the celebration of the power of music from above, has remained a symbolic tale of loss and redemption through the centuries.*

CHRISTIAN INTERPRETATIONS

The abduction of mortals by fairies, the appearance of the fairy hunt and the idea of an Otherworld that mortal men and women could travel to and return from, were all traditional motifs that appeared in Celtic folklore. At the time of the poem's composition, there were many Christian commentaries written on the original myth. One 14th-century interpretation identified Eurydice as the soul of a Christian, the king of the underworld as Satan, and Orpheus as Christ (who travelled to hell to save lost souls after his death on the Cross).

Another interpretation of the story from the same period saw Orpheus as a Christian and Eurydice as his soul; in the version in which Orpheus lost Eurydice by looking back, this interpretation said that after regaining his soul through leading a religious life and turning away from the things of the world, the Christian was tempted once more by temporal concerns and in looking back lost his soul to Satan.

CHIVALRIC MEANINGS

For the medieval audience of *Sir Orfeo*, the harp that the king played was both a courtly and a sacred instrument, and would recall the lyre played by the biblical psalmist, and paragon of chivalry, King David. Sir Orfeo's withdrawal into the forest was suggestive for the audience of a religious retreat or pilgrimage – indeed, after his temporary abdication, the king wore pilgrim robes; moreover, the fact that Sir Orfeo was granted a glimpse of Heurodis (on the fairy ride) while he was on retreat rather than on a quest would suggest the grace of God in granting spiritual benefit to pilgrims.

In addition to supporting such a religious interpretation, *Sir Orfeo* could be understood in the light of the code of

chivalry and of courtly love. The knight's loyalty to his lady, tested to the utmost limit when he gave up his worldly pre-eminence and lived in the wilderness of the forest for ten years, proved that he was worthy of her love. He demonstrated great bravery in his journey to the unknown faery Otherworld, and his prowess (in this case with the harp rather than lance or the mace) won him his reward. In addition, he proved himself a worthy ruler, putting his people in the care of a trusty steward, and arranging for them to elect a new king if necessary.

ARTHUR AND THE KNIGHTS OF THE ROUND TABLE

King Arthur and the knights of the Round Table at Camelot were honoured in the Middle Ages as the epitome of chivalry. The knights who took inspiration from the medieval cycles of Arthurian romances sought to emulate the deeds of Sir Lancelot or Sir Galahad, while many kings, princes and lords used the Round Table as the model for the organization of tournament knights or chivalric brotherhoods. As early as 1223 the Crusader knight John of Ibelin, Lord of Beirut, used the deeds of the knights of the Round Table as an inspiration for a 'Round Table' of jousting in Cyprus. Knights looked on Camelot with pride, admiration – and sadness, for the golden age of King Arthur contained within it the seeds of its own decline and failure. The medieval romances told of the great adventures of Arthur's knights, but also of the adulterous love between his queen, Guinevere, and his most trusted knight, Sir Lancelot. Their treachery, combined with the chivalric quest for the Holy Grail – the cup used by Christ at the Last Supper – led to the dissolving of the Round Table fellowship, Arthur's death and the passing of his glorious kingdom. Taken as a whole, the romances – and the wider body of Arthurian legend – were coloured with a deeply affecting elegiac tone, the sense that all great things, such as the age of Camelot, must pass away.

▲ *The Lady of the Lake meeting Guinevere, from 'The Story of Lancelot'.*

◄ *The Round Table – at which no knight could claim precedence – was presented as the ideal organization for a body of brave warriors, but when the knights departed on the Grail quest the brotherhood of fellow knights was fractured.*

LORD OF CAMELOT

KING ARTHUR'S HISTORICAL ROOTS AND THE GROWTH OF HIS LEGEND

In the great body of medieval literature celebrating Arthur and his knights, the king was cast in a number of roles – as squire called to greatness, noble ruler, peerless warrior, perfection of knighthood and the emblem of a perfect past who might one day return to lead his fallen people into a glorious future. The origins of this figure, whose appeal endures to this day, are found in an uncertain blend of Celtic history and legend.

ARTHUR'S GRAVE

Medieval knights in England were in no doubt that King Arthur was part of their history. In the 12th century a search was mounted for his place of burial.

The familiar tales of his life told that he was carried away for burial on the Isle of Avalon. This has been associated with St Michael's Mount, a sea island just off the coast in Cornwall, and L'Ile d'Aval off the coast of Brittany, but a parallel tradition, current from the early 11th century, held that Avalon was Glastonbury Tor, a hill that looked like an island among the water meadows of Somerset before the meadows were drained.

In the time of Henry II of England, Henry de Blois, abbot of Glastonbury in 1126–71, ordered a search of the Tor for Arthur's remains. Reputedly a coffin was found buried in the hillside inscribed with the legend *Hic jacet sepultus inclitus rex Arthurus in insula Avalonia* ('Here is found the grave of King Arthur, buried in the Isle of Avalon'). In the 13th century the remains were reburied in front of the high altar in Glastonbury Abbey, in the presence of King Edward I. They were visited by pilgrims until well into the Tudor era.

HISTORICAL ROOTS

Most modern historians believe that the legend of King Arthur grew up around the military achievements of a minor British or Welsh prince of the 5th or 6th century, who led a united resistance to the invasions of the Saxons. He may have been the leader of a British army that won a celebrated victory over the Saxons at 'Mount Badon' in *c*.500.

The earliest references to Arthur are Welsh. He was named in poems of the late 6th century by Welsh poets Aneirin and Taliesin, which praised his bravery and referred to him as the 'great holder of feasts'. In the *Historia Brittonum* (*History of the Britons*) of *c*.830, the Welsh monk Nennius catalogued no fewer than 12 battles in which Arthur fought the Saxons, and mentioned the great victory at Mons Badonicus (Mount Badon); in the following century the anonymous chronicler of

▲ *In his youth Arthur thought himself a mere squire, but without knowing it he was, in fact, a prince, destined to wear the crown.*

the *Annales Cambriae* ('Annals of Wales') stated that Arthur won a battle at Mount Badon in 516 but was slain in fighting at Mount Camlann in 539. The Annals also mentioned that a warrior named Medraut (a Latin form of Mordred) met his end in this fateful battle. Arthur's name appeared in 11th- and 12th-century Welsh accounts of the lives of the saints, in which he was portrayed as a great warrior.

Mount Badon is identified by many historians as the hill fort of Little Solsbury Hill near the city of Bath in southern England. Archaeologists have uncovered evidence that the fort was in use by the British at the close of the 4th century. Other theories hold that Camlann, the proposed place of Arthur's death, might

▼ *Glastonbury Tor, proposed as the site of the Isle of Avalon, takes its name from the Celtic word (tor) for a cone-shaped hill.*

be in northern England at Bidoswald in Cumbria, which was called Camboglanna in the Roman era.

ARTHUR THE BEAR GOD

Other historians, however, disagree that there was a single historical figure at the heart of the Arthurian legend. Arthur's name may mean 'bear man' from the Welsh *art* ('bear'), and some experts argue that Arthur was originally a Celtic bear god who was given a historical setting in legends. Others suggest that the name may have been a *nom de guerre* adopted by a succession of war leaders who fought against invaders.

THE LEGEND IS BORN

The legend of Arthur developed in Welsh folklore and early romances. Perhaps the earliest of these was *Culhwch and Olwen* (11th–12th century), which described Arthur as the leader of a band of heroes (forerunners of the knights of the Round Table) and placed his court at Kelliwic ('forest grove') in Cornwall; this has been identified as Callington (near Launceston) or as Castle Killibury, a hill fort near Wadebridge in North Cornwall.

The Arthurian legend was established by Geoffrey of Monmouth in his *Historia Regum Britanniae* (*History of the Kings of Britain*) in *c*.1135–39. In his fictionalized account, which was highly influential across Europe, many now familiar elements of the Arthurian cycle were present: the magician Merlin gave the British King Uther Pendragon the appearance of Gorloise, Duke of Cornwall, so that Uther could satisfy his desire to sleep with Ygerna, Gorloise's beautiful wife; as a result of this union, Arthur was born; he became king when his country was at the mercy of Saxon invaders, but drove them back decisively; he married the beautiful Guinevere and his rule was a golden age of peace and chivalry. But Camelot could not last forever: when the Roman Emperor Lucius Tiberius demanded that Britain pay tribute, Arthur travelled to France to defeat a Roman army, leaving the country

▲ *A stained glass window depicts King Arthur beside his foremost knight, Lancelot.*

in the care of his nephew Mordred; ungrateful and unchivalrous, Mordred seduced Guinevere and seized the throne. Arthur returned and killed Mordred but was fatally wounded in the last battle, at Camlann, and his body was borne off to the Isle of Avalon (which Geoffrey said meant 'island of apples').

THE ROUND TABLE AND THE GRAIL QUEST

The Anglo-Norman author Wace of Jersey translated Geoffrey of Monmouth's *History* into French as the *Roman de Brut* (1155). This work was the first to describe the round table at King Arthur's court. The French author Chrétien de Troyes, author of five Arthurian romances (*c*.1165–80), introduced the theme of the quest for the Holy Grail, the cup used in the Last Supper, which Christ had supposedly given to Joseph of Arimathaea who had brought it to Europe.

The legend was further developed in French romances of the 13th century, which added the narratives of Arthur's childhood and how his destiny as king was revealed when he drew the sword Excalibur from the stone; of the liaison between Guinevere and Arthur's most trusted knight, Lancelot; and of Lancelot's son, Sir Galahad, whose purity allowed him to succeed as far as possible in the Grail quest. These legends were made available to English audiences by the 15th-century knight Sir Thomas Malory in his *Le Morte d'Arthur* (*c*.1470).

In the development of the Arthurian legend, very little changed in the main story between Geoffrey of Monmouth and Sir Thomas Malory. One key change came with the development of the code of chivalry and theories of knighthood: Arthur himself, a warrior in the early legends and in Geoffrey of Monmouth's account, became a more courtly figure, a chivalric patron and lord of the Round Table, rather than a knight finding sport in tournaments and on the battlefield.

A KING BETRAYED

SIR TRISTAN AND LADY ISEULT

Sir Tristan was the hero of a Celtic legend about a warrior's love affair with his lord's wife. This was recast in the 12th century by Anglo-Norman poets within the conventions of courtly love, then assimilated in the first quarter of the 13th century into the cycle of Arthurian romance, so that Sir Tristan became a knight of the Round Table, where he was a rival of Sir Lancelot and participated in the quest for the Holy Grail. The story of Tristan's joyful but doomed adulterous love affair with Iseult, wife of King Mark of Cornwall, came before and probably influenced the narrative of Sir Lancelot's affair with Guinevere, wife of King Arthur.

TRISTAN'S CELTIC LEGEND

The earliest surviving versions of the story of Tristan and Iseult are in the Old French poem *Tristan* (*c.*1155–60), by Anglo-Norman poet Thomas of Britain, and the 12th-century Norman poem *Tristan* by Norman poet Béroul. An earlier story in Celtic folklore, from which all later versions were derived, is now lost but can be reconstructed with confidence.

▲ *Returning from Ireland with Lady Iseult, Sir Tristan mistakenly drinks the potion that makes him risk all for his lady's love.*

According to this version, Sir Tristan was a knight in the service of his uncle, King Mark of Cornwall, and was himself prince of the kingdom of Lyonesse. He was Mark's champion, and after defeating an Irish knight named Marhaus in a duel, was sent to Ireland to seek the hand of Princess Iseult on Mark's behalf.

In Ireland Sir Tristan killed a dragon that had been terrifying the local population, then set sail for Cornwall with the princess. On their journey they mistakenly drank a love potion that Iseult's mother had prepared for her daughter to share with Mark, and were swept away by a deep love that could not be denied.

Iseult married King Mark, whom both she and Sir Tristan liked and honoured, but secretly she carried on her love affair with Tristan. Mark was suspicious and many times tried to catch the lovers out, but they used trickery to maintain an appearance of innocence.

Finally Mark had proof of his suspicions, and sent Tristan to death at the stake and Iseult to a leper colony. But Tristan made a miraculous escape by leaping from a clifftop chapel and rescued Iseult, and the lovers took refuge in the forest of Morrois, where they lived a life of simple fulfilment.

There Mark discovered them again, sleeping naked together with a drawn sword laid between them. Shortly afterwards, remarkably, the three made peace: Iseult returned to Mark's court as his wife and Tristan departed for Brittany, where he married a second Iseult, 'for her name as well as her beauty' – Lady Iseult of the White Hands, the daughter of Duke Hoel of Brittany.

The story ended in tragedy, however: Tristan fought Morholt, uncle of the original Iseult (of Ireland) and although he performed heroically and killed Morholt, he was stabbed with a poisoned spear in the struggle; only Iseult of Ireland knew the magic to draw this poison and save his life, so he sent for her from his sickbed with the message that if she could come she should sail in a ship with white sails, whereas if she could not come the ship should sail with black sails.

Tristan called out to his wife, Iseult of the White Hands, from his bed to tell him whether the ship was coming, and she, jealous of his undying love for her rival, lied to him, telling him that the ship had

---

PAS DE LA JOYEUSE GARDE

▲ *René d'Anjou, Duke of Anjou was a chivalric legend in his own lifetime. The epitomy of a knight, he excelled in all the necessary skills and accomplishments.*

Typical of the elaborate 15th-century *pas d'armes* devised to dramatize scenes from the Arthurian cycle was the *Pas de la Joyeuse Garde* held in Anjou in 1446. A castle was built from wood near Saumur in imitation of the 'castle of love' in which, according to various versions, both King Arthur and Queen Guinevere and Tristan and Iseult took refuge. The pageant included two 'Turks', two real lions, a company of musicians mounted on horseback, a dwarf and Duke René d'Anjou on a horse led by a maiden. The best jouster won a gold clasp adorned with rubies and diamonds.

loved both Iseult and Tristan as nephew and wife; and Iseult loved Mark as her husband. Typically in the earlier versions, with the strongest influence of the magical elements in Celtic folklore, Tristan and Iseult were viewed as being under the power of the love potion and so not morally responsible for their adultery.

In the prose romance versions of the story, however, Mark became a villain who raped and murdered his niece and killed his brother Baldwin. He also slew Tristan – in this version, Tristan did not die in Brittany, but at King Mark's court: the king crept upon him and stabbed him while the knight played his harp beneath a tree.

RETURN FROM EXILE

In some versions Tristan returned from exile to visit Iseult. Two 12th-century poems, now known as the *Folie Tristan*, told of how the knight came back to King Mark's court disguised as a fool or madman, while another called the *Luite Tristan* recounts how he made his return in the guise of a minstrel. The 12th-century poet Marie de France told in her lay *Chèvrefoil* (*Honeysuckle*) of how Tristan signalled to Iseult by leaving out a hazelnut branch inscribed with the legend *Ni moi sans vous, ni vous sans moi* ('I cannot live without you, nor can you live without me').

hoisted black sails. So Tristan, believing himself abandoned by his one true love, turned to the wall and died.

When Iseult of Ireland arrived, and discovered Tristan was dead, she was inconsolable – and herself died in a final embrace with her lover. Two trees, one honeysuckle and one hazel, were planted on the lovers' grave, and their branches intertwined as a symbol of their undying love: although King Mark tried three times to cut and separate the branches, they grew back and linked once more so he allowed them to grow.

PRINCE OF LOTHIAN?

Tristan's name (which also appears as Drystan or Drustanus) was a common Pictish name, while his kingdom of Lyonesse may be a transcription into French of Lothian (a region in south-east Scotland, once part of Pictish territory). King Mark of Cornwall was a historical figure who ruled in the early 6th century, and it is possible that the legend of Tristan grew up around a historical Pictish prince

▲ *The legend of Tristan and Iseult's doomed love has inspired many reworkings. German composer Richard Wagner's opera* Tristan und Isolde *was first performed in 1865.*

who was sent to the Cornish court. Another theory is that Lyonesse refers to the Isles of Scilly off south-west Cornwall.

The earliest versions of the Tristan legend probably had no connection to the Arthurian legend cycle. However, the names of Tristan and Iseult are found in early Welsh poems in connection with King Arthur's court: Iseult was listed as one of the key figures at the court in the 11th-century *Culhwch and Olwen*, while Tristan was identified as one of Arthur's advisers in the 12th- or 13th-century *Dream of Rhonabwy*.

In the early versions of the story, King Mark was a sympathetic character, wronged by circumstance; Mark, Tristan and Iseult all honoured one another – as in the later narrative of Arthur, Lancelot and Guinevere. Tristan loved and honoured Mark as his king and lord; Mark

▼ *King Mark was present at the funeral of Tristan and Iseult, according to this 15th-century manuscript version of the story.*

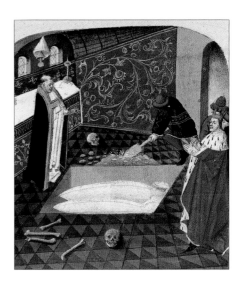

KING ARTHUR'S SENESCHAL

SIR KAY

Sir Kay was the son of Arthur's foster father Sir Ector, and so was the future king's foster brother. Kay's character differed markedly in different versions of the Arthurian legends, ranging from being one of the first and bravest of the knights of the Round Table to being a boastful fool and even a treacherous coward. He appeared often with Sir Bedivere, the knight who returned Arthur's magical sword Excalibur to the mysterious Lady of the Lake.

Sir Kay was best known in the guise presented by the French Arthurian prose romances and in Sir Thomas Malory's *Le Morte d'Arthur*. As an infant, Arthur was removed by Merlin the magician from his true parents, King Uther Pendragon and Ygrayne, and placed in the care of Sir Ector. Arthur grew up in the company of Sir Ector's son, Sir Kay, and came to serve as his squire. At a tournament in London, Arthur lost Kay's sword and thought he could replace it by drawing the magical weapon Excalibur from the stone. In so doing he revealed that he was destined to be King of the Britons. Initially Sir Kay tried to claim that he had drawn the sword himself, but in the end had to admit that it was his foster brother, Arthur, who was the chosen one. The tables were turned: Sir Kay became Arthur's squire, and then went on to serve as one of the knights of the Round Table.

A WELSH LORD, AN 'ENCHANTER KNIGHT'

Welsh folklore celebrated Sir Kay – known as Cai Hir ('Kay the Tall') – as a leading warrior with a hot temper. Some writers identify him as the 5th-century Welsh Lord of Caer Gai, who had this nickname.

The folk tales collected in the *Mabinogion* told of his great feats of bravery and chivalry. In the 11th-century tale *Cuhlwch and Olwen*, for example, Cai, Bedwyr and Gwalchmei (Kay, Bedivere and Gawain) were chosen among six champions to ride out with Culhwch from Arthur's court in Cornwall, on the quests Culhwch was set by the giant Ysbaddaden before he could marry Ysbaddaden's daughter Olwen. In the course of these adventures, Kay killed a giant named Wrnach and defeated Dillus the Bearded, making a dog's lead from his hair. Arthur made fun of his defeat of Dillus, and the two knights were briefly estranged.

In the 13th-century Welsh collection the *Triads of the Island of Britain*, Kay was celebrated as one of the three great enchanter knights of Britain. He was said to have the ability to grow as tall as a great oak, to hold his breath for nine days and nights under water and to go without sleep for the same period. He possessed a magical sword, capable of delivering wounds that would never heal, and had such bodily heat that his companions could warm themselves on his skin when the weather was cold in the wet forest – indeed when it rained, anything that Kay held would remain dry because his hand was so hot.

A CELTIC SAINT

Breton legend gave Sir Kay a further career as a hermit, churchman and saint. According to this tradition, he stood down as a knight of the Round Table in order to become the Bishop of Glastonbury. Later he went to Brittany and established a monastery there at Cléder, where a shrine was kept for centuries in honour of St Ké. He only returned to the English court in its last days when he tried without success to make peace in Arthur's war with Mordred. He also persuaded Guinevere to enter a nunnery.

A BUFFOON AT CAMELOT

In Geoffrey of Monmouth's *History of the Kings of Britain* (*c*.1135–9), Sir Kay was identified as the Count of Anjou and was said to serve as King Arthur's steward. Together with Sir Bedivere he rode out with the king to defeat the giant of Mont St Michel in Normandy. In the works of Chrétien de Troyes, however, Sir Kay was

▲ *Kay's character varied in different accounts, but he was loyal to the last. Arthur avenged Kay's murder before his own death.*

presented as a boastful and incompetent fool, a somewhat humorous figure who made fun of truly heroic knights such as Sir Lancelot or Sir Gawain, and who himself proved incapable of great deeds. In Chrétien's poem *Lancelot, le Chevalier de la Charrette* (*Lancelot, the Knight of the Cart*), Sir Kay persuaded Arthur to allow him to attempt the rescue of Guinevere when she was taken captive by Sir Meleagant. He failed, and ended up in prison, setting the scene for Sir Lancelot's triumph. In the tournament held at Le Hem, Picardy, in 1278 and described in the poem *Le Roman du Hem,* the participating noblemen took the roles of Arthurian knights and one played Sir Kay as boastful buffoon.

SIR KAY THE MURDERER

From Chrétien de Troyes' time onwards, Sir Kay was often presented as a fool and braggart, but he was only once a villain – in the early 13th-century French romance *Perlesvaus*. In this narrative, Kay killed Arthur's son Sir Loholt in an attempt to take the credit for Sir Loholt's slaying of a giant, but was found out when Sir Loholt's head arrived at court in a box that would only open to his murderer. Banished from Camelot, he sided with Arthur's enemies Sir Meliant and Brian of the Isles.

SIR KAY'S DEATH

The main tradition held that Sir Kay died as a loyal knight in King Arthur's service. According to Geoffrey of Monmouth, Sir Kay was killed while fighting the fictional

Roman emperor Lucius Tiberius in France, and the French prose romances likewise suggested that he met his end in Arthur's war in France against the Romans. Welsh sources reported that Sir Kay was slain by one of Arthur's enemies, Gwyddawg, and that Arthur, enraged at the death of his foster brother, avenged the murder.

▲ *Kay breaks his sword at a tournament. He was diminished by being transformed from the enchanter of the Welsh sources to a middling knight in the Arthurian romances.*

▼ *According to Chrétien de Troyes, Lancelot succeeded where Kay had failed in rescuing Guinevere from Meleagant's castle.*

THE MARRIED KNIGHT ERRANT

SIR EREC'S CONFLICT BETWEEN MARRIED LIFE AND CHIVALRY

Sir Geraint, also known as Erec, was one of the first knights in Arthurian romance to embark as a knight errant on a journey of chivalric encounters. These marvellous adventures included combats against magical foes, visits to spellbound castles and intense jousts with unknown knights, events that inspired jousts of war and stately *pas d'armes* tournaments in the 14th and 15th centuries. By tradition Sir Geraint, variously said to be a Welsh knight or a king of Dumnonia (roughly Devon and Somerset), was famous for his great prowess in tournaments. He even won the hand of his wife, Lady Enid, at a tournament.

EREC AND ENIDE

As Sir Erec, Geraint was the hero of the first romance written by the great French poet Chrétien de Troyes, *Érec et Enide* (*c.*1170). This 7,000-line poem in Old French, called a 'tale of adventures' by its author, predates all other Arthurian romances – save perhaps the Welsh tale *Culhwch and Olwen*, which although it survives only in 14th-century manuscripts has been dated in its original form (now lost) to the 11th century. Chrétien's romance described the conflict experienced by Sir Erec between married love and the call of chivalry.

SHAMED BY SIR YDER

At the start of the story, Sir Erec – who was not wearing armour – attended on Queen Guinevere while the other knights of the Round Table rode through the forest hunting a stag. Guinevere and Sir Erec were approached by a knight named Sir Yder, accompanied by a dwarf, who treated Sir Erec discourteously before riding off. Guinevere, feeling slighted by the insult to her serving man, ordered Sir Erec to follow him and avenge the slight.

On this adventure Sir Erec rode to a far-off town where he met the Lady Enid, whose father was the archetype of a poor knight, a warrior blessed with honour and prowess but who had lost his title and worldly wealth; Sir Erec fought in the knight's old and rusty armour at a great tournament, where he defeated Sir Yder, who was competing in disguise as the 'Sparrow Hawk Knight', and made him beg for Guinevere's forgiveness. Sir Erec married Lady Enid.

MARRIAGE PROBLEMS

Sir Erec and Lady Enid settled into a happy marriage. However, Lady Enid became distressed to hear rumours accusing Sir Erec of losing some of his knightly stature because of his attachment to her and their marriage. His companions felt he was becoming soft, and failing in his duties because he was neglecting the life

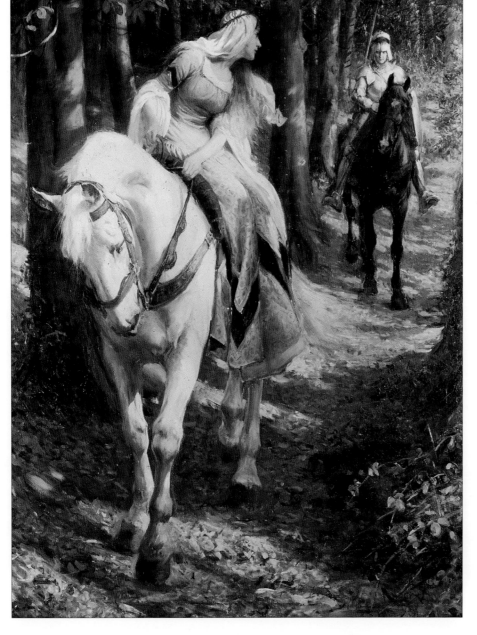

◄ Lady Enid leads the way on Sir Geraint's rather unusual chivalric quest. At the end of their adventure, they settled at Camelot.

▲ *English poet Alfred, Lord Tennyson made Lady Enid and Sir Geraint the subject of one of his first four Arthurian poems, published as* Idylls of the King *in 1859. He celebrated their faithfulness in marriage.*

▶ *On their travels there is a marital power struggle between Erec (Geraint) and Enid, which is happily resolved at the end of their journey, with each taking their natural place in the partnership.*

CELTIC ORIGINS

The same story was told in the Welsh romance *Geraint mab Erbin* (*Geraint, Son of Erbin*), which survives in a 14th-century manuscript associated with the *Mabinogion*. Some historians argue that Chrétien's poem and the Welsh romance were both based on a common Celtic original, others that the Welsh poem was derived from Chrétien's work. Geraint was a well-known figure in Welsh and Celtic folklore and romance, where he appeared as King of Dumnonia (a Celtic kingdom in south-west England that included Devon and Somerset). In some versions he was said to have died fighting alongside King Arthur against the Saxons at the Battle of Llongborth; his death in this battle (perhaps in *c*.500) was lamented in the poem *Elegy for Geraint*, which celebrated

the speed and strength of Geraint's horses and named Arthur as 'emperor'. Other Welsh sources identified Sir Geraint as one of three great 'seafaring knights' in Britain. In Cornish legend Geraint was buried on Carne Beacon close to the village of Veryan in the Roseland Peninsula, Cornwall, and was celebrated as the patron saint of the village of Gerrans, near Falmouth.

of tournaments and chivalric sports in order to spend time with his wife. Erec found Enid weeping over these rumours, and he suspected that she no longer loved him, and even that she had been unfaithful to him, and at once ordered her to prepare for a journey in his company.

They set out on a series of adventures during which he was able to prove again his prowess as a knight and she was able to demonstrate her continuing love for him. He treated her roughly and ordered her to be silent throughout the quest, but she often disobeyed his command in order to save him from dangers. At the end, after he had fought no fewer than three giants, they returned to their original home in King Arthur's court and settled back into a life of great domestic happiness.

JOUSTERS AS KNIGHTS ERRANT

At Sandricourt in September 1493 Louis de Hédouville organised an Arthurian *pas d'armes* set in a series of locations taken from romance narratives: one part of the entertainment took place at a 'dangerous barrier', another at a 'dark crossing of ways', another in a 'thorny field', another in a 'forest wilderness'. The tournament featured ten defenders taking on all-comers. The defenders were reported to have taken up their positions 'like knights errant in search of adventures'.

▼ *The Arthurian legends were rich in mysterious settings of the kind used for the Sandricourt tournament. On one of his quests, Sir Lancelot rode into a magic wood.*

THE HOLY KNIGHT

SIR PERCEVAL

Sir Perceval was a knight marked by a profound – almost childlike – innocence. Raised away from courtly civilization, in the forest, he left his home to prove himself a knight and, after achieving great feats of chivalry at Camelot, became one of the knights of the Round Table. Set aside from the other knights by his innocence, he embarked on a sacred journey in search of the Holy Grail, the cup or dish used by Christ at the Last Supper before his crucifixion, said to be imbued with miraculous power.

The narrative of Perceval and the Grail quest first appeared in the late 12th century in Chrétien de Troyes' poem *Perceval, ou Le Conte du Graal* (*Perceval, or the Story of the Grail*), written in 1181–91. Chrétien wrote the poem towards the end of his life, and it was unfinished, ending after only 9,000 lines. But such was its popularity that four later authors wrote further sections – known as the 'Four Continuations' – that altogether added an extra 54,000 lines to the poem.

▼ *The Welsh romances that fed into the Perceval story weighed the qualities of courtliness and worldliness a knight might need to acquire during his rise to greatness.*

THE KNIGHT WITHOUT COURTESY

According to Chrétien's version, Perceval was raised in the forests of Wales by his mother, who had fled civilization following the death of her husband. When some knights rode by, Perceval was awestruck by their splendid appearance, and decided to become a knight himself. Ignoring his mother's pleas to remain, he rode to King Arthur's court, where he was knighted.

Sir Perceval was taunted by the foolish Sir Kay, then set out on a series of adventures, determined to make his name. He rescued a princess named Blanchefleur from a besieged castle, and received instructions in the ways of knighthood from Sir Gornemant. He quickly picked up the necessary physical skills, but because of his lack of a courtly education he was wanting in sophistication and the chivalric quality of courtesy; Sir Gornemant ordered him not to ask so many questions.

▲ *In some versions of his legend, Perceval married a maiden he had rescued, and fathered two sons; in others, he was devoted purely to the quest for the Grail.*

FIRST GLIMPSE OF THE GRAIL

This instruction had major consequences later in the adventures, when Sir Perceval reached the castle of two ailing kings set amid a wasteland. There were two kings, father and son, both crippled by being injured from the waist down; the elder was confined to the castle while the younger was able to come and go, well enough to visit the castle grounds.

Sir Perceval saw a mysterious procession in which young women and men passed before the younger king and his guests, carrying first a bleeding lance, then a pair of candelabras and finally a mysterious vessel (the Holy Grail) containing one wafer for the Christian Mass, said to be the only food that sustained the elder

CHRÉTIEN DE TROYES

The French poet Chrétien de Troyes was the author of five Arthurian romances. After *Erec and Enid* in *c*.1170, he wrote *Cligès*, in *c*.1176; *Lancelot ou Le Chevalier à la Charrette* (*Lancelot, or the Knight of the Cart*), and *Yvain, ou Le Chevalier au Lion* (*Yvain, or the Knight of the Lion*), both in 1176–81; and *Perceval, ou Le Conte du Graal* (*Perceval, or the Story of the Grail*), in 1181–91. He was one of the great poets of the medieval age, but we know very little about his life.

As his name indicates, he was from or was associated with the town of Troyes in north-eastern France. He served at the court of Marie de Champagne, daughter of Eleanor of Aquitaine, in the years 1160-72, and may have been herald-at-arms there. In his later years he was associated with Count Philip of Flanders, to whom he dedicated the Perceval poem. He also wrote four poems based on the *Metamorphoses* of Roman poet Ovid (1st century AD) but only one, *Philomela*, has survived.

king. Because of Sir Gornemant's warning, Sir Perceval did not ask what the procession meant, or what the Grail was; and it later emerged that if he had asked, the old king would have been healed. Back at Arthur's court, Perceval pledged to make his way back to the mysterious castle and find the Grail and its meaning.

THE STORY CONTINUED

Chrétien's poem continued with a section describing the adventures of Sir Gawain, in this context King Arthur's best knight, but it did not complete Sir Perceval's narrative. However, in the last of the Four Continuations the story was brought to a conclusion: Sir Perceval achieved his quest, the Grail King died and Perceval was crowned king in his stead, then after a rule of peace and prosperity lasting

seven years, Perceval returned to the woods, living as a hermit until he died. The poet suggested that on his death he took the Holy Grail with him to Heaven.

There were many other versions of the story. In later material, Sir Perceval was secondary to Sir Galahad in the Grail quest, but still retained a key role: with Sir Bors, he accompanied Sir Galahad in the final stages of the sacred quest, reaching the castle and achieving completion.

PERCEVAL WITHOUT THE GRAIL

The Welsh romance *Peredur ab Efrawg* (*Peredur, son of York*), which survives in two 14th-century manuscripts, told much of the same story about a knight raised in the woods and embarking on a long series of adventures in which he learned how to be a knight, but it left out the matter concerning the Holy Grail. It is possible that the Welsh romance and Chrétien shared a common Celtic or Breton source. There were various possible historical prototypes for Peredur – including a Welsh king of Gwynedd mentioned by Geoffrey of Monmouth and the Welsh Triads as fighting in the Battle of Arfderydd in AD573.

The Welsh romance told the same story as Chrétien up to Perceval's stay at King Arthur's court and his shaming by the boorish Sir Kay (here called Cei). Then, embarking on his adventures, Perceval met two uncles. The first trained him in knighthood, just as Sir Gornemant did in the other account, while the second was the equivalent of the crippled king: he also showed Sir Perceval a mysterious procession of objects, but instead of the Holy Grail he revealed a man's decapitated head on a platter. After an encounter with the Nine Witches of Gloucester, meeting his destined love, Angharad Golden-Hand, and many more adventures, Sir Perceval discovered that the decapitated head was that of his cousin and took vengeance upon his killers. The romance ended with celebrations of Sir Perceval's heroism. A Middle English romance, the 14th-century *Sir Perceval of Galles*, also omitted the Grail material from Percival's adventures.

▼ *Pre-Raphaelite painter Arthur Hacker makes the innocent Sir Perceval completely oblivious to temptations of the flesh – and even gives him a halo.*

A MYSTICAL JOURNEY

SIR PERCEVAL AND THE SPIRITUAL QUALITIES OF KNIGHTHOOD

Chrétien de Troyes' poem *Perceval, or the Story of the Grail* (c.1181–91) was the direct inspiration for the masterpiece *Parzival*, written c.1200–10 by German poet Wolfram von Eschenbach. *Parzival* and other later versions of the Grail legend, such as those in the 13th-century Prose *Lancelot* and Sir Thomas Malory's *Le Morte d'Arthur*, developed the spiritual and mystical elements of the narrative and presented Sir Perceval either as himself the purest embodiment of Christian chivalry, or as one of the great examples of religious knighthood alongside Sir Galahad.

ORIGINS OF THE HOLY GRAIL

In Chrétien de Troyes' poem the spiritual element of the Holy Grail was not well developed, for Chrétien did not explain clearly what the sacred object was. It is probable that the mysterious vessel derived from Celtic folklore about magical cups and cauldrons. Examples include the legend of Bran the Blessed, who possessed a cauldron that had the power to

▼ *Sir Galahad achieves a vision of the Holy Grail while Sir Bors and Sir Perceval look on. This is one of six tapestry designs on the Grail quest created by artist Edward Burne-Jones for Stanmore Hall.*

bring the dead back to life, and Welsh tales in which Arthur and his knights made a voyage in search of a magical cauldron – in one case searching in Ireland, in another looking in the Celtic spirit world.

The Grail may also have been intended as a Christian symbol from the beginning. At around the time that Chrétien wrote his Grail poem, the Church was promoting the ceremonial and mystical aspects of the sacrament of the Mass or Holy Communion – which certainly had its origins in the time of Christ, and was practised by the early Church in the first centuries AD, but was being celebrated with new ceremony in the 12th century – and this probably lay behind the development of the Christian interpretation of the Grail as the cup or plate that was used by Christ in the Last Supper with his disciples before the crucifixion.

In the late 12th-century verse romance *Joseph d'Arimathie* (c.1191–1202) – written just after Chrétien's Grail poem – French poet Robert de Boron described how Christ gave the cup from the Last Supper to Joseph (in the Christian Gospels, a wealthy man who allowed his prepared tomb to be used for the burial of Christ after the crucifixion), and how Joseph used the vessel to catch some of

the 'holy blood' from Christ's body. After Christ's resurrection, Joseph received instruction in the mysteries associated with the cup, and later travelled to Europe where he established a line of 'Grail-keepers' to look after the vessel.

SIR PERCEVAL'S CHIVALRIC AND SPIRITUAL EDUCATION

In *Parzival*, Sir Perceval was educated first in the ways of chivalry and of courtly love. He gradually overlaid his country upbringing with chivalric sophistication – symbolized by his winning a superb suit of red armour in a tournament outside the gates of Nantes, then riding off wearing the armour with his simple country clothes beneath.

Later, after his failure to ask the necessary question at the Grail castle, he went through a prolonged spiritual education, passing through guilt and despair, discovering a deep humility and learning from a holy man named Trevrizent whom he met on Good Friday, the day of Christ's crucifixion. So prepared, he was ready to meet and fight his half-brother Feirefiz (the pagan son of Perceval's father by an early marriage to a Moorish queen in Africa, explained at the beginning of Wolfram von Eschenbach's poem). The

▲ *On the Grail quest, Sir Perceval, Sir Bors and Sir Galahad encountered Perceval's sister Amide, who nobly sacrificed herself to cure a lady of leprosy.*

two knights fought without knowing each other's true identity, and Sir Perceval's sword broke, so that he was at the mercy of his opponent, but he was spared by the noble pagan and, making friends, they discovered that they were also brothers. They then proceeded together on the search for the Grail, and finally Sir Perceval was sufficiently prepared to ask the required question of the crippled king and complete the quest.

SIR PERCEVAL'S WIFE AND SONS

According to Wolfram von Eschenbach's version, Sir Perceval married the maiden he rescued from the besieged castle (Lady Blanchefleur according to Chrétien; Lady Condwiramurs according to Wolfram) and had two sons with her, Kardeiz and Lohengrin. In a version of the medieval legend of the 'Knight of the Swan', Lohengrin was also a Grail knight and was sent in a boat pulled by a swan, to rescue a maiden who was not permitted to ask

his name. In Wolfram's poem, Sir Perceval was reunited with Lady Condwiramurs at the conclusion of his quest.

In other later versions of the Grail romance, however, Sir Perceval was presented as a virgin whose quest for the Grail ended in his death. The Grail quests replaced the adventures of knights within the courtly love convention – where the knight was seeking to do great deeds in order to win fame and the acclaim of his lady – with a spiritual search for salvation or to gain some mystical knowledge and experience of God.

SYMBOLISM OF THE FISHER KING

The older and younger crippled kings in their castle, not named by Chrétien de Troyes, were called Titurel and Anfortas in *Parzival*. In many other versions they were called the Wounded King and the Fisher King: while the older king was confined to the interior of the castle, the younger one went fishing in the water near the castle. The character of the Fisher King would seem to be based both on Celtic keepers of magic cauldrons such as Bran the Blessed and on the idea of a guardian of the Grail, developed by Robert de Boron

▲ *The Grail was carried and guarded by angels and ethereal beings. This Pre-Raphaelite portrait of one of the damsels of the Grail is by DG Rossetti.*

in his *Joseph d'Arimathie*. In Robert's romance Joseph's brother-in-law, Bron, was said to be the 'Rich Fisher' and was the first keeper of the Grail. It is possible that the name 'Fisher King' derived from a pun in French, where the words for fisher and sinner are virtually identical. There is also a link to Christ sending his disciples to be 'fishers of men'.

In the Prose *Lancelot* (the part of the Arthurian romance tradition known as the Vulgate Cycle), the two kings are called Pellam and Pelles: the second brought about the birth of the perfect knight, Sir Galahad, by tricking Sir Lancelot into sleeping with Pelles's daughter Elaine. In the still later part of the tradition called the Post-Vulgate Cycle, Sir Pellam received his wound because he fell into sin; he was injured by Arthurian knight Sir Balin, using the spear that was used to pierce Christ's side at the crucifixion. The blow that injured Sir Pellam was called 'the dolorous stroke'.

THE FLAWED KNIGHT

SIR LANCELOT

Sir Lancelot was King Arthur's greatest and most trusted knight, blessed with unmatched chivalric prowess but undone by his love for Queen Guinevere. By entering into an adulterous relationship with Guinevere, he failed his king and set in motion the events that brought about Arthur's death and the end of the golden age of Camelot.

In his earlier appearances in the Arthurian cycle, Lancelot's love for Guinevere was celebrated within the conventions of courtly love, but as the story was developed in the Prose *Lancelot*, his adultery was presented as his undoing – both as a chivalric figure and as a religious knight. In the Grail romances, Lancelot was unable to achieve success in the quest

▼ *Lancelot fell unconscious at the sight of the Grail. He was unable to complete the quest because his love for Guinevere, and subsequent betrayal of his king, gave his knightly character a fatal flaw.*

because of his illicit love for the queen, but much of his extraordinary potential was realized in his son, Sir Galahad.

THE STORY OF LANCELOT

The story, as developed by the time of the 13th century Prose *Lancelot,* told that after his father King Ban of Benoic lost his kingdom and died of a broken heart as a result, Lancelot was carried off as a boy by a water-spirit, the Lady of the Lake, who brought him up in her own kingdom. In the version told in the 12th-century German poem *Lanzelet*, this was in a magical land, where no other men were permitted, but in the Prose *Lancelot* many other fine knights lived there, including Lancelot's cousins Lionel and Bors.

When Lancelot came of age he left, bound for King Arthur's court, without having been told his name or royal background; in the *Lanzelet* he was at this stage entirely untrained in knightly pursuits, and could not even handle a horse, but in

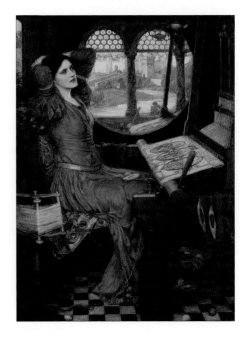

▲ *The Lady of Shalott, heroine of a work by 19th-century poet Alfred, Lord Tennyson, was based on Elaine of Astolat, who in the Arthurian legends fell hopelessly in love with Sir Lancelot.*

the Prose *Lancelot* he had benefited from a good chivalric training.

In the Prose *Lancelot*, from the moment of his arrival at court Lancelot was in love with Queen Guinevere. He rescued her from the castle of Sir Meleagant (as told in Chrétien de Troyes' poem). He recovered his father's kingdom, taken previously by the wicked Sir Claudas, but chose to live principally at King Arthur's court. At the castle of the Fisher King, he was tricked by the king into sleeping with his daughter Elaine and fathered the perfect knight, Sir Galahad. But Queen Guinevere, discovering the fact, was furious and drove him into madness and exile from Camelot.

He took part in the Grail quest, but – tainted by his sin with Guinevere – was unable to reach the end of the quest: he passed out at a mere glimpse of the Grail and remained unconscious for a length of time said to match the number of days on which he had sinned against Arthur with

▶ *One of the darker sides of the legend of the quest for the Grail was that it emptied Camelot of its knights, left Arthur's court open to attack and corruption, and caused individual self-doubt and failure.*

Guinevere. Subsequently, recovered and forgiven by Guinevere, he returned to Camelot, but then – after his love affair was betrayed to the king – he and Guinevere were discovered together by Arthur, who condemned the queen to death. Lancelot escaped and returned in time to save Guinevere, but in the battle kinsmen of Gawain were killed, sparking a long and bitter struggle between Gawain's kinsmen and Lancelot.

Finally, when Arthur travelled to France to defeat the Romans, the king was betrayed by Mordred. Lancelot took no part in this revolt, but his earlier treachery had destroyed the unity of the Round Table. Lancelot had to look on as Arthur

---

SIR HUGH DE MORVILLE

Sir Hugh de Morville, the English knight who supposedly gave Ulrich von Zatzikhoven the Anglo-Norman source for the romance *Lanzelet*, served King Richard I of England in the 1190s before standing hostage for the king. He may well be the same Sir Hugh de Morville who served Richard's father King Henry II and was one of the four knights who assassinated Thomas Becket in 1170 in Canterbury Cathedral after misunderstanding the king's forlorn complaint 'Who will rid me of this meddlesome priest?' as a command. The assassin Sir Hugh de Morville was disinherited by the king of his holdings as Lord of Westmoreland and sent to obtain forgiveness from Pope Alexander III (r. 1159–81). The pope told the four knights to travel to the Holy Land, and so perhaps Sir Hugh was on the Third Crusade with Richard I in 1189–92.

---

was killed in battle, Guinevere also died and the golden age of Camelot came to an end. He ended his life in a hermitage.

THE COURTLY LOVER

Lancelot first appeared in the Arthurian stories in the work of Chrétien de Troyes. Chrétien mentioned him in his poem *Erec et Enide* (c.1170) and made him the principal character of the poem *Lancelot, le Chevalier de la Charrette* (*Lancelot, the Knight of the Cart*), where he rescued Queen Guinevere after she had been taken captive by the wicked knight Sir Meleagant. The poem was the first to mention Lancelot's illicit love for Queen Guinevere; it was also the first to mention Arthur holding court at Camelot – although in this its first appearance, it is a minor court, less important than the king's main court at Caerleon.

Before the end of the 12th century the Swiss cleric Ulrich von Zatzikhoven developed the knight's character in his romance *Lanzelet* (c.1194), the first Arthurian work to describe Lancelot's upbringing by the Lady of the Lake. The poet wrote that his work was a translation of an Anglo-Norman work brought to Germany by the Crusader knight Sir Hugh de Morville, who stood hostage for King Richard I of England when he was captured by Holy Roman Emperor Henry VI. *Lanzelet* made

no mention of the knight's love for and adultery with Guinevere, and described his love for a princess named Iblis. It is possible that the original source legend about Lancelot was similar to that given in *Lanzelet*, and did not include the adulterous love, which would then have been added by Chrétien de Troyes, perhaps influenced by the Celtic legend of Tristan and Iseult. (Chrétien claimed that he had written a poem based on the Tristan story, but if he did it has been lost.)

A COURTLY INVENTION

Lancelot's relations with Guinevere as described by Chrétien in *The Knight of the Cart* were only comparable with those of Tristan and Iseult in the most general terms. As lovers Lancelot and Guinevere followed the conventions of courtly love whereas Tristan and Iseult's affair had far more of the magic associated with Celtic and Breton folklore. Chrétien wrote *The Knight of the Cart* for Marie de Champagne, a great patron of courtly love poems. Lancelot did not appear in earlier Arthurian material, such as Geoffrey of Monmouth's *History of the Kings of Britain*, in which Guinevere did have a lover, but he was the villain Mordred. Lancelot's story appears to have been invented with no antecedent in the Celtic legends that fed into so much of the Arthurian cycle.

THE PERFECT KNIGHT

SIR GALAHAD

In the later Grail romances Sir Galahad, son of Sir Lancelot, was the perfection of chivalry and the only knight capable of completing the Grail quest. These profoundly religious romances contrasted the religious inspiration of Sir Galahad's chivalry, based on spiritual fervour, with the courtly inspiration of Sir Lancelot's knightly achievements, which were done to impress his lady, Queen Guinevere.

Sir Galahad first appeared in Arthurian narratives in the early 13th-century *Queste del Saint Graal* ('Search for the Holy Grail'), part of the Prose *Lancelot* (also known as the Vulgate Cycle). His story was developed in the later romances of the Post-Vulgate Cycle and in *Le Morte d'Arthur* of Sir Thomas Malory.

▼ *The spear Sir Galahad carried on his sacred quest was said to be the holy lance that pierced Christ's side.*

SIR GALAHAD'S STORY

The Grail story as presented in the *Queste del Saint Graal* revealed the influence of Cistercian monks and of the mystical writings of the Cistercian St Bernard (1090–1153), founder of the great abbey of Clairvaux in France. The Cistercian ideal demanded sexual virginity for the leading heroes of the Grail narrative. As we have seen, Sir Perceval was no longer described as finding married love with Lady Blanchefleur, but was a virgin. Likewise, Sir Galahad possessed absolute purity, and was also a virgin. The stages by which Galahad rose to understanding and full vision of the Grail matched those of a mystic's movement towards realization of God, as described by St Bernard. The *Queste del Saint Graal* appears to have been written by a Cistercian clerk.

Sir Galahad was born after his father, Sir Lancelot, was tricked by magic into believing that Elaine, daughter of the Fisher King, was his beloved, Guinevere. Upon learning the truth Sir Lancelot returned at once to King Arthur's court, and when Galahad was born he was given to his great-aunt, who was an abbess. He had a profoundly religious upbringing in a nunnery. The great Merlin prophesied that Galahad would be braver even than Sir Lancelot and was the knight destined for success in the Holy Grail quest. The story stated, without giving details, that through his mother's side Sir Galahad was a descendant of the biblical King David.

Galahad was later brought to King Arthur's court at Camelot by a hermit and knighted by his father. Not knowing what he was doing, he sat down in the Siege Perilous – a magical empty seat at the Round Table that would kill any knight except the one capable of succeeding in the Grail quest. King Arthur, having knights – guided by Sir Perceval's sister – set sail across the sea, where they came to a second ship and boarded it to find the Holy Grail once more, covered and set upon a silver table.

Bors, Perceval and Galahad then sailed on to the city of Sarras, where, Christ-like, Sir Galahad healed a cripple and made him walk. The three knights were thrown in jail by the local king, but in time the king died and Sir Galahad succeeded him; then at a celebration of the Mass Sir Galahad was taken aside and shown the glorious mysteries of the Grail by a man who revealed himself to be Joseph of Arimathea. Afterwards Sir Galahad bade his companions farewell and died, and Sir Bors and Sir Perceval saw their friend's soul carried up to heaven. The Grail was taken with him.

▼ *Sir Galahad was one of several Arthurian knights raised in obscurity but destined to prove their greatness at court and on quests.*

▲ *Sir Galahad, fighting here incognito with Sir Lancelot, had the military prowess of a great knight as well as a religious seeker's determination and drive.*

witnessed the proof of Galahad's special status, gave him another test – to draw the sword from the stone. Galahad also passed this test and Arthur proclaimed him the foremost knight of all and welcomed him to the company of the Round Table. They then had a vision of the Holy Grail and Sir Galahad, Sir Bors and Sir Perceval were chosen as the best knights to pursue the quest, for Galahad had such remarkable purity of character and motive that he lived without sin.

The assembled company then retired to a meadow close to Camelot where they fought a great tournament, in which Sir Galahad, even on his first day as a knight, outdid all the other knights of the Round Table except for his father, Sir Lancelot, and Sir Perceval.

SIR GALAHAD'S SHIELD

A pure knight needed the purest weapons, hallowed by sacred history. Sir Galahad embarked on the quest carrying a shield – white as snow, with a red cross at its centre reputedly drawn in blood by Joseph of Arimathea. This shield, a red cross on a white background, was the one carried by the Knights Templar. Sir Galahad later acquired the sword of David.

In one version of the conclusion of the Grail quest, he travelled with Sir Bors and Sir Perceval to the castle of the Fisher King, where they discovered the Holy Grail. Galahad used the spear (which was identified as the spear used to pierce Christ's side as he hung on the cross) to cure the Fisher King.

Some versions ended at this point, with Sir Galahad being granted a vision of the Holy Grail and then being raised to heaven. Others provided further adventures overseas in the city of Sarras in the Middle East. According to this version, the

A KNIGHT STRONG AS THE SUN

SIR GAWAIN

The character of Sir Gawain, King Arthur's nephew, changed with the development of the Arthurian legends. In early literature he was a trusted knight and exemplary warrior, but by the time of Sir Thomas Malory he was a treacherous lord known for his rough treatment of women.

From the beginning Gawain was associated with women: altogether, in the various legends told of him, he had no fewer than 21 lovers. He was also the hero of a story in which he stepped forward to marry an ugly lady for whom Arthur had promised to find a husband, in return for help that saved his life, and she turned out to be a great beauty cast under a spell.

The magic of folklore attended Gawain, and some of his feats may be distantly connected to folktales about the Irish hero Cúchulainn; although possessed of extraordinary strength, he was flawed as a chivalric figure, because he did not live up either to the ideal of courtly knight or to the ideal of the religious-mystical knight.

Sir Gawain's character is a case study in a knight's maturing understanding of the meaning of chivalry: moving from celebration of feats of physical strength and

▼ In a scene based on the English poem Sir Gawain and the Green Knight, *Gawain is tempted by the wife of his host Sir Bercilak.*

▲ Gawain was renowned for his martial ability. In 13th-century romances he was often the only knight able to match a new hero, freshly arrived at court, in combat.

martial endeavour, to praise for courtesy and the ability to thrive, as Sir Lancelot did, within the convention of courtly love, to reverence for humility and purity as embodied by Sir Galahad.

THE HISTORICAL GAWAIN

Sir Gawain's legend appears to have grown up around the life of a late 5th-century Welsh king, Gawain Gwalltafwyn. In the Arthurian narratives, however, he had Scottish roots, as the son of King Lot of Orkney and Lothian. His connection to Arthur was through his mother Morgause, Arthur's half-sister. Gawain's brothers were Sir Agravain, Sir Gaheris, Sir Gareth and Sir Mordred. In some accounts, but not in the early Welsh Arthurian legends, Sir Mordred was the product of Arthur's incestuous liaison with his half-sister.

A CELTIC SUN GOD?

In Malory and in a number of the romances, Sir Gawain's strength grew greater and less in the course of the day –

often it was said that he was three times stronger at noon than in the evening. For this reason, it has been suggested that he was based on a Celtic sun god. In early Welsh versions of the Arthurian legends, Gawain was known as Gwalchmei. He appeared with Cai and Bedwyr (Sir Kay and Sir Bedivere) in the 11th-century *Culhwch and Olwen*, where he was King Arthur's nephew and one of his foremost knights, who was selected to travel with Culhwch on his quest.

In the following century Geoffrey of Monmouth's *History of the Kings of Britain* presented Sir Gawain as one of the leading warriors of Arthur's court, who served as the ambassador to Rome. William of Malmesbury described Sir Gawain as an enduring foe for the Anglo-Saxons, although he was finally driven from the kingdom by the brother of the semilegendary Anglo-Saxon king, Hengest. William also recorded that Gawain's grave had been discovered in south-west Wales.

WORLDLY KNIGHT

In the romances of Chrétien de Troyes, Gawain was one of the most prominent of Arthur's knights, but was often compared unfavourably with Sir Lancelot or Sir

Perceval. With the development of the Grail theme, Gawain was increasingly presented as lacking in the necessary spiritual qualities for the mystical quest – brave and forceful he might be, but too reliant also on his own strength and unable to understand the significance of the Grail.

HATRED FOR SIR LANCELOT

In the romances of the Vulgate Cycle (*c*.1210 onwards) Gawain played an important role in the end of the Round Table fellowship. He refused to take part when his brothers Agravain and Mordred exposed the secret love of Sir Lancelot and Queen Guinevere to King Arthur, but after Arthur had condemned his wife to death and Sir Lancelot returned to rescue Guinevere, a battle broke out in which all the brothers save Mordred were killed. Gawain's respectful friendship with Sir Lancelot became an implacable hatred that was the bitter backdrop for the final days of Camelot. In this version Gawain lost his life fighting against Mordred and before he died wrote to Lancelot asking for his forgiveness.

Sir Gawain's character had been transformed into a villain and even a murderer by the time of the Prose *Tristan* and the Post-Vulgate Cycle romances (both written *c*.1240). In his *Le Morte d'Arthur* (*c*.1450–70) Malory reproduced the largely negative image of Sir Gawain presented in the French romances.

ENDURING ENGLISH POPULARITY

Yet more positive images of Sir Gawain survived and endured: the English poem *Sir Gawain and the Green Knight* (*c*.1375) presented Gawain as a brave and loyal knight. His popularity endured: the story of his encounter with the Green Knight was retold in a rhyming romance of *c*.1500, and we know from a description by courtier Robert Laneham that a minstrel performed a Gawain romance as part of the festivities laid on at Kenilworth Castle in 1575 for Queen Elizabeth I.

The story of *Sir Gawain and the Green Knight* was based on an old folkloric nar-

▲ Sir Gawain and Sir Yvain failed in the Grail quest. In one story Gawain saw the chalice but allowed himself to be distracted by the beauty of the maiden carrying it.

rative of a beheading game, which was told of heroes including Cúchulainn. At Camelot when the court was celebrating New Year's Day a knight dressed in green armour arrived unannounced and proposed a game: he would allow anyone to strike him with an axe if the person agreed to the Green Knight returning the blow in one year's time. Sir Gawain took up the challenge and decapitated the knight. But after receiving this blow the knight stood and picked up his own head; before leaving, he instructed Sir Gawain to meet him at the Green Chapel in one year's time.

One year later, searching for the Green Chapel, Sir Gawain came to a fine castle and was welcomed by its lord Sir Bercilak and his ravishing wife. Sir Bercilak embarked on a hunt and proposed a deal with Sir Gawain: he would give Sir Gawain whatever game he caught while Gawain would give the lord whatever he gained during the day. When he was gone, the lady of the castle visited Sir Gawain's chamber to try to seduce him, but he resisted her advances, only allowing her to give him one kiss; in the evening, he gave the kiss to the lord. On the second day, the same thing happened, but the

lady gave two kisses; Sir Gawain later passed these on to Sir Bercilak. On the third day the lady gave him three kisses and a green girdle that she said would keep him safe from physical harm; in the evening he gave the three kisses to Sir Bercilak but withheld the girdle.

The following day being New Year's Day, Sir Gawain met with the Green Knight at the Green Chapel, wearing the girdle. The Green Knight swung his great axe three times, only injuring Gawain slightly on the third swing. He revealed himself to be Sir Bercilak, and said that he would not have hurt Sir Gawain at all had he been honest about the girdle; they had, he said, been taking part in a game arranged by the sorceress Morgan le Fay. Sir Gawain returned to Camelot wearing the green girdle as a sign of his shame at having been outwitted, but King Arthur on hearing the tale announced that all the knights of Camelot should henceforth wear a green sash in honour of Gawain.

A VILLAIN AT CAMELOT

SIR MORDRED AND OTHER KNIGHTS

The Arthurian court of legend had a large supporting cast of lesser knights. The principal of these must be the traitor Sir Mordred, the antithesis of chivalry. Others included Sir Bedivere, one of the king's earliest companions, and the paragon of purity Sir Bors the Younger, who played an important role in the quest for the Holy Grail.

ARTHUR'S NEMESIS

Sir Mordred was King Arthur's nemesis, the traitor son who rebelled against his king, bringing about the Battle of Camlann at which Arthur was fatally wounded and in which Sir Mordred himself lost his life. In some versions of the legend, King Arthur and Sir Mordred were the last two warriors left alive at the end of the Battle of Camlann and settled their dispute in single combat: Arthur killed Sir Mordred, but not before he had been fatally wounded himself.

▼ *Mordred was the worst of rebels – a son (and/or nephew) who turned against his father or uncle. At the Battle of Camlann he fought Arthur in single combat.*

Sir Mordred was either Arthur's illegitimate son by his half-sister Morgause, or (in earlier traditions) Arthur's nephew and the legitimate son of Morgause with her husband King Lot of Orkney. The theme of Mordred's birth as a result of Arthur's incest was introduced in the 13th-century Prose *Lancelot* (the Vulgate Cycle). The

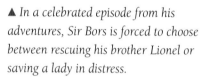

▲ *In a celebrated episode from his adventures, Sir Bors is forced to choose between rescuing his brother Lionel or saving a lady in distress.*

story went that Arthur discovered what he had done, and heard a prophecy that a baby born on Mordred's birthday, May Day, would bring him and his kingdom low. He rounded up all the babies born on that day and set them in a boat at sea, but he could not escape his destiny, for although the ship sank, Mordred survived and was washed ashore.

Sir Mordred first appeared as Sir Medraut in the 10th-century *Annales Cambriae* ('Annals of Wales'), where he was said to have died at the Battle of Camlann, with Arthur. In various Welsh legends, Sir Medraut was a raucous and violent man – in one story he rode to Arthur's court at Kelliwic in Cornwall, consumed all the drink and food, pulled Guinevere from her throne and beat her. In Geoffrey of Monmouth's account, he was a traitor, who rebelled when Arthur had to leave his kingdom to fight the father's kingdom and raised with their cousin Lancelot by the Lady of the Lake.

Sir Bors was often tempted by maidens to abandon his vows of chastity. In one episode, he was approached by a fair lady who threatened to kill herself if he would not sleep with her; he refused, and the lady and her maidens were revealed to be demons. He did father one son, Sir Elyan the White, when he was tricked with a magic ring into making love to Lady Claire, the beautiful daughter of King Brandegoris of Estangore. Sir Bors the Younger survived the collapse of Camelot. According to legend he embarked on a Crusade, and was killed fighting in the Holy Land.

Romans in France and this set the tone for his role in the whole body of Arthurian literature. He was often described seducing or even raping noble ladies, and fighting their husbands.

SIR BEDIVERE THE STRONG

One of King Arthur's unfailingly loyal knights, Sir Bedivere was celebrated for his strength. His Welsh name, Bedwyr Bedrydant, meant Bedivere of the Immaculate Sinews, and it was said that although he had only one hand, he could still fight more swiftly and skilfully than any other warrior.

With Sir Kay and Sir Gawain, he was among the earliest known knights of King Arthur's court – listed, as we have seen, in the 11th-century Welsh tale *Culhwch and Olwen*. He was usually associated with Sir Kay, and fought with him and King Arthur in defeating the Giant of Mont St Michel in Brittany. In Geoffrey of Monmouth's account, Sir Bedivere was King Arthur's head butler and also Duke of Normandy.

BEDIVERE AND EXCALIBUR

Sir Bedivere was also the knight charged with returning the sword Excalibur to the Lady of the Lake as Arthur lay dying (see box). The story suggested that Sir Bedivere, with a very human response, found it difficult to cast so precious a

▲ *Fatally wounded in the Battle of Camlann against his rebel son, Mordred, Arthur fell into the sleep of death. On the Isle of Avalon attendants guard his passing.*

weapon into the water, and tried to trick his lord in order to keep the sword: he twice returned to the king's bedside and reported that he had thrown the sword away into the water as instructed, and when Arthur asked what had happened Sir Bedivere reported that it had slipped into the water and disappeared; Arthur knew he was lying and scolded him. The third time, when Bedivere at last threw it in, the hand of a mysterious lady emerged from the water, caught it and drew it under. Subsequently, following Arthur's death, Sir Bedivere retired to a hermitage, where he spent the rest of his life.

SIR BORS THE YOUNGER

The antithesis of Sir Mordred was Sir Bors the Younger, who was celebrated for his purity of character. He was even able to see the Holy Grail. He was the only knight to return to Camelot after the Grail quest.

Sir Bors was called the Younger because his father, another Bors, also had a part in the Arthurian legend. Sir Bors the Elder was king of Gaunnes (Gaul) and uncle to Sir Lancelot. Bors the Younger and his brother Lionel were exiled from their

KNIGHTS IN HISTORY

In November 1095 at the Council of Clermont in France, Pope Urban II issued the call to arms to Christian knights that resulted in the First Crusade. To stir up enthusiasm for a war against Muslims in the Holy Land, he held up the example of the great Frankish king Charlemagne and his knights, whose military encounters in Spain and southern France with Islamic warriors from the Iberian Peninsula and northern Africa were already celebrated, in works such as the epic Anglo-Norman poem the *Chanson de Roland* (*Song of Roland*), as great feats of war against Muslims. Urban's speech, which had such momentous consequences, is an indication of how literary tales of chivalry were intertwined with the historical deeds of knights.

The *Song of Roland* and other *chansons de geste* – songs celebrating the great figures and heroic exploits in the era of Charlemagne – were the first flowering in a long tradition of poetry and romances that wove colourful legends of chivalry around the past adventures of knights. These works, whose accounts of chivalric deeds were strongly influenced by legend, presented exemplary images of knighthood that were held up by Urban and others as an inspiration for the knights of their day. In addition, the accounts in the poems and romances were to some extent determined by the prevailing culture – in particular, they often filled a need for 'crusading propaganda', showing knights fighting heroically for Christ and their Muslim foes acting with dishonesty and cowardice.

▲ *An imagined joust between Richard I and a blue-skinned General Saladin.*

◄ *Charlemagne was said to have 12 paladins or leading knights – just as Christ had 12 disciples. This ceiling fresco of the great king is from the Palace of Justice in Paris, France.*

CHRISTIAN KNIGHTS IN BATTLE

ROLAND, CHARLEMAGNE'S FIRST KNIGHT

The *Song of Roland* is the earliest surviving example of the Anglo-Norman and French *chansons de geste* ('songs of heroic deeds'), epic poems that celebrated feats of arms performed by knights in the service of Charlemagne and other Frankish kings. It is the oldest surviving epic poem in French and because of its quality as well as its antiquity enjoys a preeminent place in medieval literature. Traditionally the poem was seen as a French work, but recent scholars have established that it belongs in the Anglo-Norman tradition.

The poem survives in a number of manuscripts, the oldest of which dates to *c.*1130–70, but it was composed by the time of the First Crusade and perhaps even earlier: according to the 12th-century Anglo-Norman poet Wace, at the Battle of Hastings in 1066 Duke William of Normandy's minstrel performed the poem before the battle. This claim (made in his *Roman de Rou*, *c.*1160) and Pope Urban II's reference to Charlemagne and his knights at Clermont in 1095, indicate that the *Song of Roland* and perhaps other chansons about Charlemagne in the late 11th century already enjoyed wide currency as celebrations of Christian knights at war. Although no chansons survive from before the mid-12th century the poems were probably passed down orally and may have been developed 100 or even 200 years before they were written down.

CHARLEMAGNE AND MARSILIUN

The *Song of Roland* tells the story of the downfall and death of Charlemagne's favourite knight. The emperor was 36 when he led a short and largely unsuccessful campaign in Spain in AD778. In the poem, however, his army brought the whole of Muslim Spain under Christian control, save only the city of Saragossa; Charlemagne, moreover, was said to be 200 years old, a grizzled veteran of wars fought in God's name.

Marsiliun, the Muslim king of Saragossa, sent a message to Charlemagne saying that he would come to the French king's court at Aix for the festival of Michaelmas, would accept the Christian faith, and give Charlemagne hostages. His plan was to trick Charlemagne into returning to France, and he had no intention of honouring his promise: he would be happy to lose the hostages if it meant that Charlemagne was no longer threatening his city. Charlemagne accepted the offer.

THE TREACHERY OF GANELON

Charlemagne sent a message of acceptance through Roland's stepfather, Ganelon, who was jealous of Roland and plotted to bring about his downfall. Ganelon proposed a deal to Marsiliun: he would arrange for Roland and his friend Oliver to be in charge of the small rear section of Charlemagne's army, and Marsiliun could lie in wait for them in the mountains and defeat them. If he killed Roland, nothing would upset Charlemagne more.

Ganelon arranged it as he promised. Charlemagne was troubled by bad dreams, and was concerned that his beloved Roland would be vulnerable in the weak rear section of the army, so he made him promise to summon help with his horn if he needed it. The Muslim army attacked

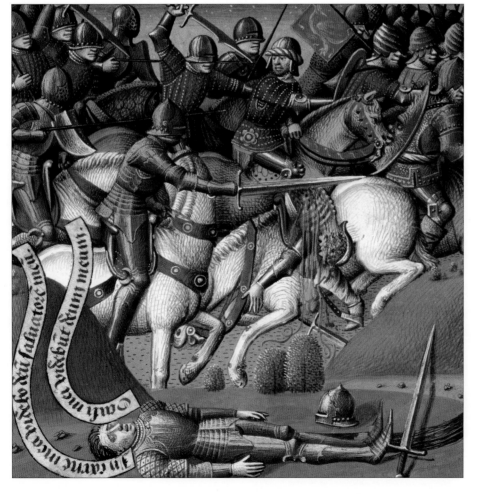

◀ *Even the great must die. In this illustration from* The Mirror of History *by the 13th-century Dominican friar Vincent of Beauvais, the Battle of Roncesvalles rages while Roland's body is stretched out in death beside his sword.*

fiercely. Oliver urged Roland to blow the horn, but Roland refused, saying that a call for help would be shameful.

PASSAGES OF ARMS ON THE BATTLEFIELD

The poem presents the encounter between the armies as a series of individual combats between knights: in the first attack 11 Christian knights, including Roland, were victorious, while only one Muslim warrior, Margarit of Seville, triumphed. However, in the second attack, most of the Christian knights were laid low. Then Roland sounded his horn. Far ahead, beyond the Pyrenees in France, Charlemagne heard the call and ordered the front section of the army to mount and return to the pass.

But it was too late. On the battlefield only 60 Frankish knights were left alive. Oliver was mortally injured in one encounter, and having lost his sight, mistakenly attacked Roland with his great sword Halteclere. Roland identified himself and absolved Oliver, for he could see that he was dying. One by one the Christian knights died. Roland made sure

▼ *This image of Roland sounding his horn to summon the help of Charlemagne and the rest of the army is from a 13th-century German edition of the poem.*

that none of the Muslims could get their hands on his famous sword Durandel by arranging his body on top of it as he prepared for death. He died unconquered in spirit, asking God for forgiveness with his final breath.

AFTER THE BATTLE

Charlemagne and the Franks defeated the remaining Muslim forces. They marched home to France, carrying the bodies of Roland, Oliver and Archbishop Turpin, and buried them at Blaye, near Bordeaux. In Aix Charlemagne ordered the execution of the traitor Ganelon.

At the end of the poem, Charlemagne was called once more to holy war: the Archangel Gabriel visited the king in his bedchamber and demanded that he take his army to the aid of a certain King Vivien besieged by pagans in the city of Imphe. Charlemagne was deeply reluctant to agree to the angel's demands, and tore his beard, bemoaning his fate, but he knew that it was his duty to fight for Christianity and to turn back the infidels.

THE HISTORICAL BATTLE OF RONCESVALLES

We know nothing for sure about the Battle of Roncesvalles. Charlemagne certainly led a military campaign in Spain in 778, but the famous battle in the Pyrenees might never have taken place. If it did happen, it was probably a minor skirmish that was developed in legend and literature as a major chivalric event.

The earliest reference to Charlemagne's 778 campaign in Spain was broadly contemporary with the events, in the Royal Annals of his reign, but made no reference to a battle at Roncesvalles. However, when around a quarter of a century later the annals were revised, an account of an attack on the rear of his army in the Pyrenees was added.

Einhard's biography of Charlemagne, the *Vita Karoli Magni* (*Life of Charlemagne*), written in *c.*817–30, described the events as a minor defeat but named Hroudland, or Roland, as one of those killed. By *c.*840,

▲ *In northern Europe Roland became a symbol of the independence of cities from the nobility. Statues of the hero were raised in many squares – as here in Riga, Latvia.*

when a biography of Charlemagne's son Louis was written, the author not only mentioned the battle but also commented that the names of the men who died at Roncesvalles were so well known that they need not be mentioned; clearly the legend of the conflict and its aftermath was firmly established by this point.

If the battle did occur, we do not know whether Charlemagne was attacked by Basques or Muslims or by a combined army of both. In Spain, Charlemagne's troops had razed the city of Pamplona before heading northward through the Pyrenees, bound for France; perhaps the Basques wanted revenge for this act, and so launched a raid. Some accounts, on the other hand, suggested that Charlemagne had taken the emir of Barcelona hostage, and it may be that Spanish Muslims attacked the Frankish army in an attempt to avenge this act.

IN SEARCH OF GLORY

WILLIAM OF ORANGE, KNIGHT OF CHARLEMAGNE

One cycle of *chansons de geste* told of the heroic deeds of William of Orange, a knight in the service of the great Charlemagne. The poems celebrated in particular his battles against the Saracens in southern France.

THREE CYCLES OF CHANSONS

Chansons de geste were traditionally grouped in three cycles, according to a classification proposed by the trouvère Bertrand de Bar-sur-Aube in the first lines of his chanson *Girart de Vienne* in c.1180. The first cycle was the *Geste du roi*, songs principally about Charlemagne, including the *Song of Roland*. The second was the *Geste de Garin de Monglane*, a group of chansons mainly about William of Orange. The third cycle was the *Geste de Doon de Mayence*, about rebellions against the king's authority.

WILLIAM OF GELLONE

There were 24 chansons in the *Geste de Garin de Monglane* cycle, dating from the 12th–15th century. The cycle was named after the primarily legendary warrior Garin, and the hero of the poems was his great-grandson William – who was based on a combination of historical figures.

The main model was William (or Guihelm) of Gellone. As one of Charles Martel's grandsons, he was cousin to Charlemagne; under the king's patronage he was made count of Toulouse from AD790 to 811, and he took Charlemagne's son Louis the Pious into his household for his chivalric education. William was an obdurate opponent of the Muslim 'Saracens' of Spain on their incursions into southern France. In 793 he won a great victory over a Muslim army at the Roman city of Orange in southern France – this was celebrated in the 12th-century chanson *La Prise d'Orange* (*The Taking of Orange*) and his achievement won him his nickname as 'William of Orange'.

He fought the Saracens again at Villedaigne, and was defeated. This defeat, renamed the Battle of Aliscans and cast in heroic-elegaic light in the manner of the *Song of Roland*, became the subject of a whole series of treatments in the cycle of poems – including *La Chanson de Guillaume*, *Aliscans*, and *La Chevalerie Vivien* (see below).

Despite the upset at Villedaigne, William's manoeuvres drove the Islamic army to retreat to Spain; in the same campaign, however, another branch of the Saracen forces established a garrison at Narbonne. In 803 William campaigned in northern Spain and helped in the capture of Barcelona from the Muslims.

In 806, like many heroes of chivalric literature, he retired from life in the field to live as a monk in a monastery that he had founded at Gellone near Lodève. He made a gift to the monastery of a relic said

▲ *William of Orange and other paladins of Charlemagne were steadfast opponents of Islam in France and Spain. This illustration shows Turks and Moors regaining territory during the long struggle.*

to be a piece of Christ's cross, which Charlemagne had reputedly been given by the patriarch of Jerusalem and had passed on to William. He died in the monastery in 812 or 814, and was later sainted. The monastery became a major pilgrimage site for religious travellers bound for Santiago de Compostela.

WILLIAM OF PROVENCE

Another model for William was the 10th-century nobleman William I, Count of Provence, who decisively defeated Saracen raiders from Fraxinetum at the Battle of Tourtour in 973. The Saracens at Fraxinetum were pirate-raiders from

▲ *Louis I the Pious, son of Charlemagne, features often in the background to the chansons of Garin de Monglane.*

around the Mediterranean, who had been making inroads into southern France and northern Italy; the war of 973 began after the raiders took captive the abbot of the monastery of Cluny and demanded a ransom. William went on to take the Saracen base at Fraxinetum and drove the raiders right out of southern France. He was hailed as 'the Liberator' and 'Father of the Country'. Like William of Gellone, he subsequently retired from military life to become a monk.

THE BATTLE OF ALISCANS AND ITS AFTERMATH

In the poems William was celebrated as the paragon of feudal warriors, a loyal supporter of Louis the Pious. He took as his wife a Saracen sorceress, Orable, who converted to Christianity and accepted the name Guibourc.

The central episode in the William of Orange poems celebrated a chivalric defeat at the Battle of Aliscans (thought to be based on the Battle of Villedaigne, which was actually fought alongside the river Orbieux in south-western France but in the poem was relocated to an old Roman cemetery near Arles, farther east). The episode concerned William's beloved nephew Vivien, who – like Roland – failed to summon his uncle's help in battle against a great Saracen army until it was too late; William rode on to the battlefield with a great army, but was himself defeated and then had to go home alone, with all his great knights cut down. This was described in *La Chanson de Guillaume* (*The Song of William*).

Another chanson, *Aliscans*, described how William had his revenge for this defeat, with the help of Guibourc's brother, a huge kitchen servant named Rainoart who fought with a wooden yoke used for bearing buckets of water. The chanson *La Chevalerie Vivien* explained Vivien's defeat by revealing that he had taken a vow never to retreat by even a single pace in battle, and had deliberately provoked an attack at Aliscans by killing an entire boatload of Saracen raiders. The battle was thought a fitting subject for chivalric literature for many years – the great 12–13th century German poet Wolfram von Eschenbach, author of *Parzival*, did his own version in the poem *Willehalm*.

YOUTHFUL EXPLOITS AND INHERITANCE TROUBLES

Two poems, *Les Enfances Guillaume* and *Les Enfances Vivien*, described the youthful exploits of the men who became these great knights. It was a convention to describe the youthful achievements of knights either in a separate *enfances* poem or in a section of a longer work. Another chanson, *Les Narbonnais*, relates the *enfances* of all seven sons of William's father Aymeri of Narbonne. This chanson is interesting for casting light on the reality of land inheritance difficulties: Aymeri passed his land to his youngest son (rather than his oldest, as he would have done in reality) and the other six had either to conquer territories for themselves or to find paid employment at the court of the great Charlemagne. The poem ended with the six older sons riding in to drive off a besieging Saracen army at Narbonne.

AYMERI OF NARBONNE

One part of the cycle was based on the adventures of William's father, Aymeri of Narbonne. The poem *Aymeri de Narbonne* recounted how he captured Narbonne from the Saracens and was given feudal rights there as seigneur by Charlemagne. It also details his marriage to Ermenjart, sister of the king of the Lombards, and their many children – the fifth of his daughters was named as Blanchefleur and was said to be the wife of Charlemagne's son Louis the Pious.

▼ *Louis the Pious fought alongside William of Orange in one of his campaigns against Spanish Islam, leading an army to attack the city of Barcelona in 803.*

REBEL LORDS

CHANSONS DE GESTE CELEBRATING KNIGHTS IN REVOLT

The third main cycle of *chansons de geste*, the *Geste de Doon de Mayence*, celebrated the campaigns of feudal lords against royal authority. The main heroes of the poems were Ogier the Dane, the four sons of Duke Aymon, and Duke Huon of Bordeaux.

The cycle took its name from Doon de Mayence, whose character was probably developed late in the series to provide a heroic ancestor for the other lords. The chanson devoted to Doon de Mayence described his childhood and *enfances* ('youthful exploits'), then gave an account of the lord's rebel fighting in Saxony, which probably had a basis in history. There was also a tantalizing reference in the *Chronicle of Fredegar*, a history of the Franks for the years AD584–641, to a revolt by warriors of Mayence against King Sigebert III of Austrasia, in his war against Duke Radulph of Thuringia in 640.

In the poems the lords all rebelled against Charlemagne, but his name was used in place of that of other less celebrated kings, both earlier (such as Sigebert), and later (such as his son Louis the Pious, and Louis's successors).

▼ *In this illustration from Renaud of Montauban, Charlemagne is seen receiving the homage of his knights after battle.*

OGIER THE DANE

In the chanson *La Chevalerie Ogier de Danemarche*, Ogier was a Danish prince who had a son killed by Charlot, one of Charlemagne's sons, and rose in revolt. He killed Charlot and was only just stopped from killing the king himself. He then fought Charlemagne for seven years, but finally made peace in order to join the Frankish king in a war against the Saracens. In this conflict he killed a giant named Brehus.

Historians believe that Ogier was probably based on a Danish king, Godfred, who fought against Charlemagne's expansion in the north of Germany at the start of the 9th century. In Danish folklore Ogier became a major figure, with a stature like that of King Arthur; he is said to be sleeping in his castle at Kronborg, ready to return and fight when his nation needs him.

THE COLOURFUL ADVENTURES OF RENAUD OF MONTAUBAN

One of the most popular poems of the cycle was *Les Quatre Fils Aymon* (*The Four Sons of Aymon*), also known as *Renaud of*

▲ *In the chanson* Les Quatre Fils Aymon, *Maugis used his sorcerer's powers to overcome a serpent and win the enchanted horse Bayard.*

Montauban. It survives in a manuscript from the late 12th century, but it is possible that older versions have been lost. It described the rebellion of the four sons of Duke Aymon of Bordeaux – Aalard, Guichard, Renaud and Richard – which began when they accidentally killed Charlemagne's nephew Bertolai at the great king's court at Aachen and had to flee for their lives.

At first they took refuge in the Ardennes, described in the poem as an enchanted forest, where they built a great fortress named Montessor. Charlemagne, driven by his desire to avenge his nephew, tracked the rebels down and captured Montessor. The four lords escaped once more and lived for seven years as bandits in the countryside.

They were joined by their cousin Maugis, who was a sorcerer. Renaud then came to the aid of King Yon of Gascony in driving back an invasion by a Saracen army, and was rewarded with the hand in marriage of Yon's sister Clarisse. He built another fortress, Montauban.

Charlemagne arrived at Montauban in the company of the great Roland himself. Then Renaud, with the help of Maugis, disguised himself and on his great horse Bayard managed to outrun Roland in a horse race before seizing Charlemagne's crown and fleeing.

The horse Bayard was an important character in the poem, and enjoyed a prolonged popularity in other chivalric legends and poems. The horse had the power to change its size according to the size of its rider, and could carry all four sons of Aymon at once.

Many further adventures ensued with the brothers always following the code of chivalry, no matter how difficult things were; at one point they were so short of food and drink that they had to drink Bayard's blood to survive. Eventually, they made peace with Charlemagne. Under the terms of the agreement, Renaud travelled with Maugis to the Holy Land and helped the crusaders to capture Jerusalem; Charlemagne took possession of Bayard and ordered that the animal be thrown into a river with a millstone around its neck. But Bayard survived and went on to be reunited with Renaud.

Then Renaud returned to France, before in traditional manner renouncing the military life to live as a religious hermit. He found time to travel to Cologne and helped to build the superb cathedral there (the Gothic cathedral was begun in 1248 on the site of an earlier Christian building that had burned down). However, Renaud was killed in a quarrel with other stonemasons.

REBELS AGAINST AUTHORITY

The character of Charlemagne in *Les Quatre Fils Aymon* was treacherous and committed to seeking vengeance for wrongs done, and the poet made a good deal of the king being outwitted by the sorcerer Maugis. But throughout all the adventures, feudal authority was upheld.

Of course revolts against feudal rule were by no means uncommon, even within ruling families. King Henry II of England, for instance, faced two revolts by his own sons and his queen, Eleanor of Aquitaine. In the first in 1173, he emerged victorious, but the second in 1189 proved to be the end of him. Tradition has it that it was the discovery of the involvement of his favourite youngest son, the future King John of England, that broke Henry's heart and sent him to his deathbed. He died, breathing these bitter words at his last: 'Shame, shame upon a vanquished king.'

DUKE HUON OF BORDEAUX

Colourful legend and the romance of the Orient, doubtless as reported by crusaders, entirely swamped historical fact in the late 12th-century chanson about Duke Huon of Bordeaux. Duke Huon was another lord who reputedly killed Charlemagne's troublesome son, Charlot, which led Charlemagne to set Huon a romantic quest: he must find his way to the court

▼ *Maugis and Queen Isanne, surprised in her bedroom by intruders in an illustration from the chanson* Maugis d'Aigremont.

of Sultan Gaudys, the admiral of Babylon, and there decapitate the Sultan's most celebrated guest, plant three kisses on the Sultan's daughter, and pluck hairs from the sultan's beard and four teeth from his mouth as trophies.

Huon set out with several knights in his company. He went first to Jerusalem, and prayed before Christ's tomb, then travelled in the company of a French penitent named Gerames through an enchanted forest ruled by Oberon, King of the Fairies. Later adventures included killing the giant Angolafer before they arrived at Babylon, which was presented as a city on the river Nile, in Egypt.

Huon succeeded in his first two tasks, then was cast in to a dungeon. The sultan allowed him out to fight and defeat another giant, Agrapart, brother of Angolafer, then laid on a banquet. This descended into a full-scale battle between the Sultan's Muslim knights and Duke Huon's Christian knights, who were helped in their hour of need by Oberon and a fairy host. Huon retuned to France, where Oberon reconciled him with Charlemagne. On Oberon's death, Huon succeeded him as king of the fairies.

GERMAN KNIGHT AT COURT

SIEGFRIED AND THE *NIBELUNGENLIED*

The dragon-slaying warrior Siegfried, fearless hero of the German epic poem the *Nibelungenlied* (*Song of the Nibelungs*) of *c*.1200, was primarily based on a mythical character from German and Norse oral legend and folklore. In the *Nibelungenlied*, this ancient legend was overlaid with historical material, and the Siegfried of the poem is thought to have been based on famous figures from the era of the Frankish kings and earlier.

HISTORICAL BACKGROUND

The destruction of the Nibelungs (or Burgundians) described in the poem may be based on the defeat of the Burgundian kingdom by the Roman general Flavius

▼ *Siegfried's great reputation as a warrior, and his many heroic feats, including the slaying of a dragon, persuaded Princess Kriemhild to accept him as her suitor and, ultimately, her husband.*

Aetius and an army of mercenary Huns at Worms in AD436 when approximately 20,000 Burgundians were reputedly slaughtered. There are other relevant historical events; one is the marriage of Attila, King of the Huns, to Ildikó, a Burgundian princess, in the middle of the 5th century. Another possible influence for the tale is the feud that arose between the Merovingian queens Brunhilda and Fredegunde in the 6th century, which was so fierce that each woman persuaded her husband to go to war against the other.

One possible model for Siegfried was a Merovingian king of the Franks of around AD600. Another much earlier archetype could be Arminius, leader of the Germanic Cherusci tribe from the northern Rhine, who in AD9 fought in scale armour as he led a coalition of Germanic tribes to a famous victory over three Roman legions in the Battle of Teutoburg Forest, a victory whose fame rang down the ages.

▲ *Known as Etzel in the* Nibelungenlied, *Attila, King of the Huns from 434 to 453, is referred to as Atli in the Icelandic sagas.*

ANCIENT LEGENDS IN A COURTLY SETTING

The *Nibelungenlied* recast the Germanic-Norse folklore and historical elements within the setting of Christian knighthood and the conventions of courtly love, in much the same way that Welsh legends about King Arthur were reinvented for a courtly audience in the works of Chrétien de Troyes and others. However, although Siegfried, while he was courting Kriemhild, behaved in accordance with the courtly love conventions, the poem also displayed violent emotions and an emphasis on revenge that was more at home in older legends and folklore than in courtly love literature.

SIEGFRIED IN THE *NIBELUNGENLIED*

Siegfried, a German prince from Xanten on the lower Rhine, arrived at Worms to woo Kriemhild, the Burgundian princess and sister of King Gunther. Kriemhild, however, was resolved not to wed after she had a violent dream, which her mother interpreted as meaning that any man she married would meet a bloody end. A retainer of King Gunther, named Hagen, related Siegfried's many great feats including the killing of a dragon and his winning of a great treasure from brothers Schilbung and Nibelung. With King Gunther's permission, Siegfried led the Burgundian army in a war against the Danes and Saxons, and his heroism in battle helped to soften Kriemhild's feelings for him.

Then news arrived that a queen of wondrous beauty and martial strength named Brunhilde had offered to wed the knight who was capable of defeating her in conflict. King Gunther decided to send Siegfried, but used magic to make him invisible; while Siegfried performed acts of martial valour, Gunther would go through the motions and take the credit for Siegfried's victory. Siegfried's reward would be the hand of Lady Kriemhild in marriage. The plan worked: Brunhilde accepted Gunther as her husband, and Kriemhild wed Siegfried. But later, after a quarrel between the two wives, Kriemhild revealed the trick to Brunhilde.

Hagen then allied himself with Brunhilde to seek revenge and to protect Gunther's honour. From Kriemhild, he learned of Siegfried's only weak spot by pretending that he needed to know so that he could cover the great warrior in battle.

▲ *The water spirits of the Danube prophesy the defeat of Gunther's army to Hagen on his way to the court of Etzel.*

(After his slaughter of the dragon in his youth, Siegfried had bathed in the animal's blood and ever afterwards was invulnerable in battle – save in one tiny spot on his back, which without his knowing had been covered with a leaf from a linden tree while he was bathing.) Hagen put the knowledge to wicked use, and killed Siegfried by striking him with a spear in the vulnerable part of his back as he was leaning over a river during a hunting trip.

Siegfried was buried with great ceremony and Kriemhild, distraught with grief and brought low by mourning, lived on

in Worms. She began to distribute the treasure of her dead husband, but Hagen stole it and hid it in the river Rhine.

The remainder of the poem described Kriemhild's violent revenge against the Burgundians who had murdered her husband and stolen her fortune. She married Etzel (based on Attila, King of the Huns), hoping he would help her get revenge. Some years later, at her insistence, Etzel invited King Gunther and Hagen to his court and in a mass battle Gunther was defeated and killed while Kriemhild herself killed Hagen with Siegfried's own sword. Kriemhild was then killed by the aged knight Hildebrand, who was horrified by the violence she had unleashed.

Hildebrand, whose name meant 'battle sword', was the brother in arms of Dietrich von Bern, an archetype of the just ruler and a legendary incarnation of the historical 5th-century King of the Ostrogoths, Theodoric the Great. According to the *Nibelungenlied*, Dietrich and Hildebrand were living in exile at Etzel's court at the time, and fought with great heroism in the battle between kings Etzel and Gunther and their retainers.

◄ *The grief of Kriemhild upon the death of her love Siegfried soon turned to vengeful fury in the* Nibelungenlied. *She achieved terrible revenge with the help of her second husband Etzel – Attila, King of the Huns.*

EL CID

THE LIFE AND LEGEND OF DON RODRIGO DIAZ DE VIVAR

Legends grew up about the chivalric feats of Spanish knight Don Rodrigo Diaz de Vivar even before he died in 1099. He was Spain's greatest general of the 11th century, who fought both for the Spanish crown and for the Moors or Saracens. In his own lifetime he was known as El Campeador ('the Champion') and El Cid (derived from the Arabic title *assid*, meaning 'lord'). The heroic legend and stirring historical facts of his life inspired many ballads and chronicles about El Cid, as well as the magnificent 12th-century poem, *Cantar de Mio Cid (Song of My Cid)*.

BIRTH AND RISE TO FAME

Don Rodrigo was born at Bivar, near Burgos, in 1043 and had his chivalric education at the court of King Ferdinand I of Castile and Leon, where he rose to become commander of the royal army by the age of 22 under Ferdinand's eldest son, King Sancho II. However, when Sancho died in 1072 and was succeeded by his brother

▼ *In a celebrated incident the Cid, on behalf of the parliament of Castile, made King Alfonso VI swear that he had no part in the death of the his brother Sancho II.*

Alfonso, Don Rodrigo lost the position to Count Garcia Ordonez, who became a great rival. Nevertheless he remained at court and married Alfonso's niece Jimena, and they had a son and two daughters.

After Don Rodrigo took Count Ordonez captive in 1079, King Alfonso cast him into exile in 1081. Don Rodrigo then entered the service of al-Mu'tamin, Moorish king of Saragossa in north-eastern Spain. He fought for al-Mu'tamin, and his successor al-Musta'in II, for almost ten years, winning many victories against fellow Moors and Spanish Christian kings.

PRINCE OF VALENCIA

After being briefly recalled by Alfonso, Don Rodrigo fought on his own account to take control of the Moorish kingdom of Valencia in 1090–94. He ruled the city, nominally under Alfonso VI but in reality in his own right, governing both Muslims and Christians. He turned the city mosque into a cathedral and appointed a French bishop named Jerome. As a statement of his princely status, he was able to wed his daughters, Cristina and Maria, to, respectively, Ramiro, Lord of Monzón and Ramón Berenguer II, Count of Barcelona.

▲ *El Cid was a Christian knight equally at home in the service of Islamic kings. Castile lost a great servant when it exiled him.*

However, Valencia was not a Christian city for long. Soon after the Cid's death in 1099, the city was besieged by Almoravids (a fresh wave of Muslims who had invaded Spain in 1086). King Alfonso VI tried to save the city, but decided he could not hold it, and the city was evacuated and burned. The Cid's body was taken for burial at the monastery of San Pedro near Burgos in Castile. The Almoravids took control of the ruins of Valencia and the rebuilt city remained Muslim until 1238.

THE CID'S FIRST VICTORY

Legends about Don Rodrigo told how he first achieved notice as a great knight by defending the honour of his father, Diego Laynez: with a single blow of his sword, he defeated the knight, Don Gomez, who

▶ *El Cid defeats Don Gomez at Callaforra, avenging an insult to his father Diego Laynez. This illustration is from a 1344 manuscript of the* Chronicle of Spain.

had slighted Diego. Gomez's daughter, Ximena, married the Cid because she was so enamoured of his strength and virtue.

The legend then described a number of campaigns against the Moors, fought in the service of 'King Ferrando' (Ferdinand I), and the declaration by Ferrando – who had heard the Moors call Rodrigo 'Cid' – that the warrior should be called 'El Cid'. Subsequently, Holy Roman Emperor Henry III, with the support of Pope Victor II, demanded tribute from Ferrando, who refused. In the ensuing war the Cid beat Remon, Count of Savoy, and a French army, then went to Rome to oversee the chastened pope signing a guarantee that a Holy Roman Emperor could never demand tribute from a Spanish king.

GREAT CHIVALRY

According to legend, following Ferrando's death, while in exile, the Cid performed countless feats of great chivalry and Christian love. In one tale he was riding to Santiago de Compostela to worship at the shrine of Spain's patron saint, St James, and he picked up a leper from the roadside and gave him a ride on his great horse

▼ *A statue in Burgos shows the Cid mounted on his trusty horse, Bavieca, and brandishing his magnificent sword, Tizona.*

Bavieca. Later at the inn, he shared his table and bed with the leper, trusting God to protect him from infection. In the night he woke to find the leper transformed into Lazarus – the dead man brought back to life by Christ in the Gospels. Lazarus predicted a glorious career for the knight.

Many episodes in the ballads and chronicles and the *Song of My Cid* described the Cid's military feats in battle against the Moors, emphasizing his tactical intelligence, his magnanimity in victory, his fairness in dividing the spoils of victory among his men, his piety in diverting riches to the support of churches and monasteries, and his personal physical prowess as a knight.

Like other knights of legend, he had a magnificent sword and horse, themselves celebrated in stories. According to the *Song of My Cid*, the Cid did not acquire his horse, Bavieca, until late in his career, when he captured it from a king of Seville who had tried to take Valencia. Bavieca was unquestioningly loyal and obedient, and by tradition never accepted another

rider after the Cid's death. When the horse died it was buried opposite the monastery of San Pedro. His sword was called Tizona.

LEGENDS OF THE CID'S DEATH

The legend of the Cid's death told that the great knight, forewarned in a dream by St Peter that he was to be called to heaven, instructed his leading comrades how to fight off an impending Moorish siege of Valencia and arranged for his body to lead into battle as if he were alive. In the battle that followed it was said that 70,000 angel knights came to the aid of the Cid's men, including one who carried a flaming sword and a bloody cross. The Christians drove their foes into the sea, where their blood turned the waves red.

Afterwards, the Cid's body was again strapped to his trusty Bavieca and led back to the monastery of San Pedro de Cardena. There it was placed on an ivory throne, with the sword Tizona in its hand, and reputedly sat there for ten years. A sweet smell arose from the body – an indication that the Cid was a saint.

DEFENDER OF JERUSALEM
LEGENDS ABOUT CRUSADER KNIGHT GODFREY OF BOUILLON

Fantastical legends grew up around the achievements of the knights who retook Jerusalem on the First Crusade (1096–99), notably Godfrey of Bouillon, one of the key figures of that episode. Godfrey, second son of Eustace, Count of Boulogne, was one of the first knights to scale the walls of the city in July 1099; he refused to be declared king in the city where Christ had died and instead took the title 'Defender of the Holy Sepulchre'.

Godfrey was the hero of a 14th-century romance narrative that reworked a cycle of 11th-century *chansons de geste*, known as the Crusade cycle, and combined them with the medieval legend of the 'Knight of the Swan', telling of a sleeping knight in a swan-drawn boat who appeared to defend a lady's honour on condition that she did not ask his name. In the Arthur tradition presented by Wolfram von Eschenbach in his *Parzival*, the Swan Knight was Sir Lohengrin, son of Sir Perceval, but in the Godfrey tradition the Swan Knight was the grandfather of the crusader knight.

THE SONG OF ANTIOCH
The reworked group of Crusade chansons (not named in the categorization of songs by trouvère Bertrand de Bar-sur-Aube) included the *Chanson d'Antioche* (*Song of Antioch*), which survives in a version dating from *c*.1180, and was based on an early poem believed to have been written during the First Crusade. This original poem was reputedly composed by Richard le Pèlerin ('Richard the Pilgrim'), a poet who travelled with the crusaders and is said to have begun the poem during the siege of Antioch. The chanson contained many hyperbolic descriptions and great lists of knights' names.

The late 12th-century version of the poem was written by Graindor de Douai, author of the other two reworked poems in the cycle – the *Chanson de Jérusalem* (*Song of Jerusalem*) and the *Chanson de Chétifs* (*Song of the Prisoners* – a reference to Christian knights held by Muslims in the Holy Land). All chansons featured Godfrey of Bouillon as a central figure.

▲ *In the French version of the legend of Lohengrin, the Knight of the Swan was named Elias and married Beatrix of Bouillon, grandmother of Godfrey.*

▼ *This 19th-century painting of Godfrey, his brother Baldwin and their men crossing into Anatolia in 1097 captures the sense of exaltation among the crusaders.*

The 14th-century Godfrey of Bouillon narrative began with an account of the birth of the Swan Knight and proceeded to describe how that knight came to the rescue of the duchess of Bouillon by winning a duel against her persecutor, Regnier of Saxony. He then married the Duchess's daughter and they had a daughter named Ida, but his wife asked his true name and so the Swan Knight had to leave – afterwards it emerged that the name was Elias. Then Sir Pons and Sir Gerart, kinsmen of Sir Elias, went on crusade to Jerusalem where they met Cornumarant, Muslim king of the city.

GODFREY THE CRUSADER

Many years afterwards, Ida's three sons – Eustace, Godfrey and Baldwin – went through their chivalric education and emerged as great knights. In Jerusalem, King Cornumarant's mother had a vision in which she saw Godfrey and his kin arriving in their full glory as crusaders – and also later knights' famous conflicts with Saladin at the time of the Third Crusade. As a result, Cornumarant made a voyage to Europe to visit Godfrey, and met a whole host of great figures of the Crusades on his travels: Robert Curthose; Tancred, Prince of Galilee; Bohemond of Antioch; Adhemar of Le Puy; Raymond of

▼ *Unstained amid carnage, Godfrey leads the way into the Holy City of Jerusalem.*

Toulouse and Hugh of Vermandois. Cornumarant's plan was to assassinate Godfrey of Bouillon and so make it impossible for his mother's troubling prophecy to come true, but faced with the knight in all his glory the travelling king was unable to do the deed. In fact his presence and mention of the city of Jerusalem had the unlooked-for result of planting the idea of making a crusade in Godfrey's mind.

The next stage of the narrative was the reworked *Chanson d'Antioche*. It described Pope Urban II's preaching of the crusade, the planning and preparations among the crusaders, their farewells to those staying behind, the journey to Constantinople and then the successful siege of Antioch, which lasted for eight months.

The narrative proceeded to describe the adventures of Christian *chétifs* ('prisoners') in the company of Corbaran, the deposed king of Antioch, on his return to his homeland. It included a section in which the prisoners performed the familiar knightly feat of killing a dragon, and then one of their number, Sir Arpin of Bourges, went to the aid of King Corbaran's son in

▲ *In July 1099 Godfrey and the crusaders marched in procession around Jerusalem (in emulation of the Israelite leader Joshua at Jericho) believing the city would then fall.*

various escapades; finally the captives were released and joined the other crusaders at the walls of Jerusalem. The crusader army, led by Godfrey, survived several assaults by the Saracens; in this version, Bohemond of Taranto was fighting with the crusaders rather than looking after his own interests, at Antioch (as the historical Bohemond was doing during the siege of Jerusalem). The narrative described how the crusaders tried repeatedly to take the Holy City without success before their prayers were answered and the city fell.

The story described how even in their moment of raucous triumph Godfrey and the other leaders of the crusader army remembered their proper humility and declined to be named king in Christ's city, but God sent them a sign indicating that Godfrey should be given the honour. After the capture of Jerusalem, the narrative ended with the death of Cornumarant.

GERMAN CRUSADER

EMPEROR FREDERICK I 'BARBAROSSA'

Frederick I, nicknamed 'Barbarossa' (meaning 'red beard'), was the Holy Roman Emperor from 1152 until his death in 1190. He went on two crusades, fighting with distinction alongside his uncle, Conrad III of Germany, on the Second Crusade (1145–49), and at the end of his life leading an army of 15,000 men on the Third Crusade (1189–92). He died attempting to cross the river Saleph in Cilicia (now part of Turkey) en route to the Holy Land.

THE SLEEPING KING

Frederick Barbarossa was hailed as one of the greatest of German rulers. His deeds were celebrated in the Latin chronicle *Gesta Friderici I Imperatoris* (*Deeds of the Emperor Frederick I*), written by the Cistercian monk and bishop Otto von Friesing. Legends swiftly grew up around Frederick's name, most notably to the

▼ Because of his opposition to the papacy and efforts to impose authority in Germany Frederick was glorified in the 19th century as a symbol of German pride and unity.

effect that he did not truly die, but can be found asleep in a cave in the Kyffhauser mountain in central Germany, and will ride forth to save Germany in her hour of greatest need.

According to this legend, his red beard has grown through the table before which he sits with his eyes half-closed. He stirs periodically to send a boy out to see if ravens are still flying around the mountain, for the prophecy has established that when the ravens stop flying Germany will desperately need his help.

AUTHORITY IN GERMANY

As Holy Roman Emperor, Frederick set out to restore the empire to the greatness it had enjoyed in the time of its founding father Charlemagne, and also in the 10th century under Otto I. At the start of his reign, he sent out an order for peace in Germany and gave a number of concessions to the princes of his territory to

▲ Frederick became embroiled in a long power struggle in Italy with Pope Alexander III. Following defeat in the Battle of Legnano, he made peace with Alexander and his allies in the Treaty of Venice (1177).

achieve this. He acted vigorously and effectively throughout his reign to defuse disputes and maintain his authority. He sought to emphasize his reign's continuity with that of Charlemagne, and organized a great celebration of the canonization of the former king of the Franks at Aachen in 1165.

CAMPAIGNS IN ITALY

Frederick led six expeditions into Italy to enforce his imperial rights there. On the first he was crowned Holy Roman Emperor by Pope Adrian IV (r. 1154–59), but he later fell out with the papacy and was excommunicated in 1160. On his fourth trip in 1167 he won a great military victory over a mighty papal army in the Battle of Monte Porzio near Tusculum (in modern Lazio, central Italy). Victory opened the way for Frederick to depose the pope, Alexander III (r. 1159–81), and appoint his own candidate, Paschal III, but an outbreak of plague in the imperial army ended the campaign and sent Frederick back to Germany.

THE EMPEROR WHO CHEATED DEATH

On the fifth Italian expedition, with an army of 8,000 knights, he suffered a heavy defeat fighting the pro-papal Lombard League at the Battle of Legnano. In the heat of the battle, Frederick's guard and standard bearer were killed and the emperor himself was thrown from his horse and left for dead. The army pan- icked and fled, and knights brought the news to Frederick's wife, Beatrice, in Pavia

▼ *A monument on the Kyffhauser mountain features this 6.5m (22ft) sandstone statue of Barbarossa apparently awaking from sleep, ready to come to Germany's aid.*

that her lord had been killed. For three days, his death was mourned, but he then appeared unannounced in Pavia, having recovered from his wound sufficiently to make his own way back home from the field of battle.

THE THIRD CRUSADE

Frederick made peace with the pope before embarking on the Third Crusade. He took the cross at Mainz Cathedral on 27 March 1188, and raised a vast German army, including 3,000 knights. They set out to follow the land rather than the sea route to the Holy Land since the army was too large to go by ship.

They travelled through Hungary and Serbia and reached Constantinople in 1189. They moved on into Anatolia and in May 1190 captured Iconium (now Konya in Turkey, at that time the capital of the Sultanate of Rum). The news of the army's approach caused consternation among Muslim leaders in the Holy Land, including Saladin. The Muslims began to gather their own army in readiness for a great conflict.

▲ *A 12th-century chronicle illustration shows Frederick, enthroned, with his two sons, Emperor Henry VI and Duke Frederick V of Swabia.*

However, on 10 June 1190 Frederick fell from his horse while crossing the river Saleph and died – either because the shock of the cold water gave him a heart attack or because he was impeded so badly by his armour that he drowned in the river, although the water was said to be only waist-deep. The death of their leader caused much of the army to panic and many abandoned the crusade and headed for home.

The command devolved on his son, Frederick of Swabia, who led the remnant of the army to Antioch. His aim was to bury his father in Jerusalem, but efforts to preserve the corpse using vinegar were not successful. Barbarossa's flesh was removed from his bones by boiling at Antioch, and buried there, while the bones were carried on by the army. Further reduced by fever, the army made its way to Tyre, where Frederick's bones were buried, and then to Acre. The crusade was carried on by Philip II of France and Richard I of England, who had travelled with their armies separately from Barbarossa.

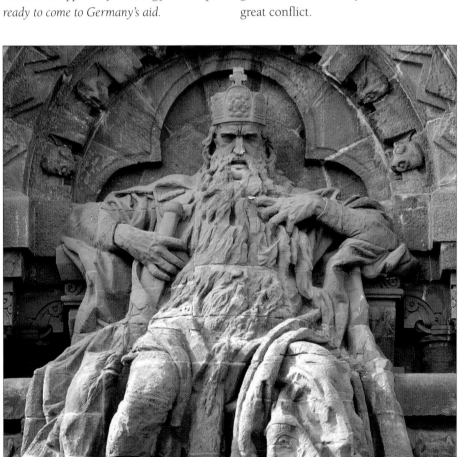

THE ROMANCE OF COEUR DE LION

COLOURFUL LEGENDS ABOUT KING RICHARD I OF ENGLAND

The legend of King Richard I of England was growing even before his death in 1199, and was firmly established by *c*.1250, when the Anglo-Norman romance of *Richard Coeur de Lion* was written. Before the end of the 13th century this was expanded into an English poem that celebrated Richard as the perfect embodiment of chivalric virtue. At this time, the romance suggests, chivalry was thought to be epitomized by a taste for combating Saracens and a love of court poetry. The Richard of the legend was also marked by a superhuman bravery.

The romance gave Richard a marvellous origin, which was typical of literature of the period but curious perhaps given that Richard's true parents, King Henry II and Eleanor of Aquitaine, hardly needed improving upon. In the poem King Henry was said to have married the fairy daughter of the pagan king of Antioch, and they had three children: Richard, John and a daughter, Topias.

▲ *Philip II of France receives a messenger and takes the cross with Richard I prior to the Third Crusade.*

One day the mother fled, because her fairy nature meant that she could not sit piously through a church Communion service. She ran from the church, carrying Topias and John, but dropped John, whose leg was broken. Richard became king and in his very first act declared a tournament, at which much bravery was displayed. He chose the two most chivalrous performers, Sir Thomas Multon and Sir Fulk Doyly, to be his close companions. (In reality, as we have seen, Richard was not a keen tourneyer, but his reign was associated with the fighting of tournaments throughout England because he introduced a system of licensing for the holding of such events.)

A TASTE FOR SARACEN BLOOD

Later parts of the romance made much of Richard's enthusiasm for killing Saracens on crusade, and described how he not only struck the fiercest warriors down but also cooked them and ate their flesh with relish. They also described an imaginary duel between Richard and the great Saracen general Saladin.

Richard was warned in a dream sent from heaven that Saladin was planning an elaborate trick: with apparent generosity, Saladin had provided his adversary with a fine horse to ride for the encounter in the lists, but in truth the horse was the son of the distinguished mare that Saladin himself was to ride. When the mare whinnied, Richard's horse would kneel in an attempt to drink its mother's milk, putting Richard at the mercy of the Saracen leader. Richard matched his opponent's cunning and took the precaution of filling his horse's ears with wax, so that when Saladin's mare whinnied it had no effect. He defeated Saladin in the encounter, but allowed him to escape with his life.

▼ *Richard and the Muslim general Saladin met in the course of the Third Crusade. An image from the English* Luttrell Psalter *(1340s) represents them jousting. Richard's face is hidden by his helmet. Both ride horses wearing elaborate caparisons.*

HOW RICHARD GOT THE NAME 'LIONHEART'

The 13th-century English *Coeur de Lion* gave a colourful account of how Richard came by his *nom de guerre*. It told how before the king ever went on crusade, when he was returning from a reconnaissance mission to the Holy Land, he was imprisoned by a certain King Modard of Germany. Richard proved a troublesome prisoner, for he killed Modard's son and made love to his daughter while in captivity, and in his rage Modard arranged for a starving lion to be released into the English king's cell.

Marked above all else by his bravery, Richard showed no fear as the lion came for him, its mouth wide open. With lightning speed, he reached down the creature's throat and tore its heart out. Then he broke out of his prison and marched into the great hall of the castle, where the king was sitting at dinner with his retainers and his fair daughter. Richard waved the bloody heart under the king's nose, then dipped it in some salt and ate it raw with apparent delight – and, as the poet noted, without bread. In awe of his captive, King Modard declared that he should be called 'Richard Lion Heart'.

▼ *Richard I's faithful minstrel Blondel hears his master's voice emanating from the dungeon of an Austrian castle where the king is held captive.*

▲ *Richard's legend emphasized his noble qualities. On his deathbed, he pardoned Bertrand de Gurdun, the young man who had fatally injured him.*

RICHARD AND BLONDEL

An often-repeated part of the legend was based on events after the crusade, during Richard's disastrous return to Europe when, after being shipwrecked near Venice, he was captured and jailed first by Duke Leopold of Austria, and then by Holy Roman Emperor Henry VI.

At the time when Richard was in Duke Leopold's dungeon, the romance said, no one at the English court knew what had become of him and Richard's favourite minstrel, Blondel, set out to search for his king. The poet wandered across all the countries of Europe and eventually arrived in Austria where he heard from a local that a great lord was imprisoned in Duke Leopold's castle. Suspecting that it might be Richard, he managed to get employment there as a musician. But he was not able to find out whether the prisoner was Richard. For many months he worked there without success, but one day he was in the garden and Richard, happening to look out of the window of his dungeon, saw him. Richard sang aloud the first verse

of a song they had composed together, and which nobody else knew, and Blondel, hearing the song, knew for sure that his lord was confined within. Shortly afterwards he left the castle and returned to England and reported to all where their king was imprisoned.

Blondel's legend grew up around the reputation of a French trouvère named Blondel of Nesle (a place near Amiens, northern France). Blondel, who reputedly got his name because he had long blond hair, was the composer of 25 songs. He was either Jean, Lord of Nesle, who like Richard fought on the Third Crusade; or his son, also Jean, who succeeded his father and fought on both the Fourth Crusade and the Albigensian Crusade. We do not know whether there was actually a connection between the historical 'Blondel' and King Richard.

A later version of the romance has a slightly different account of the Blondel legend. It suggested that the minstrel went around Europe while singing the first verse of the song that only he and Richard knew outside places where he suspected Richard might be incarcerated. Finally, when he hit upon the right place by chance, he heard Richard's voice replying from within, singing the second verse.

ADVENTURES IN LOVE AND ON CRUSADE

THE COURTLY REPUTATION OF BONIFACE OF MONTFERRAT

Boniface, Marquess of Montferrat in north-western Italy, presided over one of the most highly regarded courts of chivalry in Europe. His chivalric exploits were celebrated in song by his court poet and friend, the troubadour Raimbaut de Vaqueiras. Boniface fought against the Lombard League in Italy and Sicily, and led the Fourth Crusade in 1201–04.

Raimbaut declared that Boniface's knightly virtues were so great that they must have been bequeathed by the great figures of chivalric legend, an indication of the way in which the great figures of chivalry past and imagined were not only inspiring examples, but almost presiding deities of knighthood. Alexander the Great had given Boniface his generosity, while he had got his daring and bravery from Roland and the other 12 knights of Charlemagne. His courtesy and his charm

▼ *In the early part of the Fourth Crusade, the crusader army attacked and captured the city of Zara in Dalmatia (now Croatia).*

with the women of the court he must have got from Berart de Montdidier (who was the subject of a now lost epic poem).

PROTECTOR OF LADIES

Boniface's achievements as a young man in the 1170s, as described in Raimbaut's *Epic Letter*, were the very stuff of courtly chivalry. In one adventure, he rescued Saldina de Mar, a prominent young woman from Genoa, who had been seized by Albert of Malaspina and taken to his most inaccessible retreat. Boniface and Raimbaut rode in at suppertime and took possession of the young woman, then carried her off to her lover Ponset d'Aguilar, who was, according to the poem, expiring in his bed for love of the young lady.

The *Epic Letter* also described Boniface's rescue of the wealthy young woman Jacopina of Ventimiglia from her wicked uncle, Count Otto, who was plotting to take her money and dispatch her to Sardinia. On hearing the news that Count Otto was plotting against Jacopina, the

▲ *A near-contemporary Byzantine mosaic represents Boniface's crusader army capturing Constantinople in 1204. The mosaic is from a church in Ravenna, Italy.*

chivalrous Boniface sighed deeply, for he remembered the kiss that the lady had given him when she had asked him to protect her against her scheming uncle. He and Raimbaut, along with three other knights – Bertaldo, Guiot and Hugonet del Far – rode by night to her rescue and plucked her to safety from the quayside only moments before she was to be sent into exile.

CHIVALRIC ADVENTURES

According to the poem, they then had many adventures in her company as they rode across country, with enemy knights in pursuit. They had to go into hiding when knights rode out from Pisa to encounter them, for they were extravagantly outnumbered, and went without food or water for two days. Then they had a dramatic encounter with a group of 12 brigands at Belhestar Pass, during which Raimbaut was wounded in the neck but then was rescued by Bertaldo and Hugonet del Far.

That night, at last, they were welcomed into a comfortable home, and their host Sir Aicio was so entranced by the virtue, good looks and good standing of Boniface,

▲ In 1840 French romantic painter Eugène Delacroix painted this celebrated canvas of the crusaders' capture of Constantinople on the Fourth Crusade. The attack on the city was the culmination of centuries of ill-feeling between crusaders and Byzantines.

that, according to the poem, he wanted to give his beautiful daughter, Aigleta, to the knight as a bride. However, Boniface did not wish to enter into this arrangement, although he did subsequently arrange a marriage for both Jacopina and Aigleta, and he ensured that Jacopina's inheritance was restored to her.

Raimbaut declared that with Boniface he had worked through many dramas of courtly love. His lord had arranged at least 100 marriages for ladies who would have otherwise pined away, tying them to the most noble barons, marquises and counts; and, Raimbaut claimed, he had never given in to the temptation to lie with a single one of those needy ladies.

PROWESS IN BATTLE

These adventures were recalled in the later part of the *Epic Letter*. The earlier sections praised Boniface's exceptional prowess as

a warrior and recalled the many exploits patron and poet had shared in the field – charging and unseating foes, jousting both on bridges and in river-fords, attacking castles and clambering over sheer walls, and braving many a danger.

In 1191–93 Boniface and Raimbaut fought in Italy, on the side of the Cremona League against the League of Milan. Then in 1194 they joined in Holy Roman

Emperor Henry VI's campaign to Sicily, where at the Battle of Messina, Raimbaut came to the rescue of Boniface, according to his writings, defending his lord with his shield against a storm of javelins, swords, daggers, knives and crossbow bolts. For this timely act of bravery, Boniface rewarded his loyal friend and court poet with a knighthood.

In the *Epic Letter* Raimbaut celebrated an incident in Italy in which Boniface, with only ten companions at his side, was pursued by 400 knights but did not take flight; instead he turned on his pursuers and struck them so hard that they were overcome with fear. The poem also praised Boniface's part in the Fourth Crusade, although this was not in truth a heroic endeavour – and diverted to the sacking of Constantinople, capital of the Byzantine Empire. Raimbaut summoned a vision of this event as a great chivalric encounter, the emperor of Constantinople fleeing from the crusader army, like a thief, with 'his heart down in his heels' and the Christian army as swift as hawks chasing herons, as fierce as wolves chasing sheep.

▼ In 1201 Boniface was elected to lead the Fourth Crusade following the death of Count Theobald of Champagne, the original leader, from a mysterious malady.

SCOTLAND'S GREATEST KNIGHT

SIR WILLIAM WALLACE

Sir William Wallace is celebrated as probably the greatest chivalric figure in Scottish history, heroic leader of resistance to the English invasion of Scotland, victor against all odds at the Battle of Stirling Bridge in 1297. His feats of chivalry inspired an oral tradition of tales about him that were collected together in the ballad *The Acts and Deeds of Sir William Wallace, Knight of Elderslie,* written in c.1470 by a poet called Henry the Minstrel or Blind Harry, and other works in the 16th century including the *History of William Wallace.*

Traditionally Wallace was said to have humble origins that were contrasted with the noble family of his contemporary

▼ *A bronze statue of William Wallace stands in a niche to the right of the gatehouse at Edinburgh Castle. It is matched by a statue of another great Scottish warrior, Robert the Bruce.*

Robert the Bruce. Modern research, however, suggests that Wallace's father was a minor noble, Ayrshire knight Sir David Wallace, a landholder as vassal to James Stewart, 5th High Steward of Scotland. The name 'knight of Elderslie' referred to Elderslie, near Paisley in Renfrewshire, which was once thought to be his place of birth, in c.1270.

GUERRILLA FIGHTER

Wallace first emerged as a guerrilla fighter combating the rule of King Edward I of England, who in 1296 sacked Berwick-upon-Tweed, defeated a Scottish army at the Battle of Dunbar, forced the Scottish king John Balliol to abdicate and, in an act of extreme provocation, removed the Scottish coronation stone, the Stone of Scone, to London.

In May 1297 Wallace led a company of 30 men in an attack on Lanark in which its English sheriff, William Heselrig, was killed. Wallace went on to attack and defeat a series of English garrisons that lay between the rivers Forth and Tay. Blind Harry's ballad invented a background story to add colour to these events. According to his version, Wallace's father and brother were killed after a fight with some English soldiers, and the attack on the sheriff of Lanark was an act of revenge for the Englishman's mistreatment of Wallace's young wife Marion.

Blind Harry also introduced a scene in which Edward I put 360 Scots barons to death at Ayr by sending them on horseback through a doorway, where a noose wrenched them from the saddle and hanged them. In Harry's account, these murders later provoked Wallace to kill the entire garrison by locking the gates and setting the city on fire. He then, according to Blind Harry, led his men to Selkirk Forest to hide, and subsequently – after a tip-off about English movements – they took refuge in the Highlands.

▲ *Sir William Wallace's story, as celebrated by the minstrel Blind Harry, was based more on legend than fact. Blind Harry's ballad was the basis for the 1995 historical movie* Braveheart.

THE BATTLE OF STIRLING BRIDGE

William Wallace's finest hour was on 11 September 1297 when, despite being vastly outnumbered, a Scottish army under his command defeated English forces under John de Warenne, Earl of Surrey, in the Battle of Stirling Bridge. The Scottish force took up position on flat ground to the north of a very narrow bridge across the river Forth and were able to pick off the vanguard of the English army after it had crossed the river, while the rest of the English army was stuck on the south side of the water – the bridge was so narrow that only two knights could cross at a time.

The weight of men made the bridge collapse, meaning that many Englishmen – hampered by weapons and armour – drowned in the river. According to Blind

Harry's version, the bridge was deliberately destroyed, brought down by a Scottish freedom fighter hiding beneath it. More than a hundred English knights were killed, including King Edward's treasurer in Scotland, Sir Hugh de Cressingham. The traditional accounts told that his skin was tanned and used to make belts and sporrans by the Scots, amid wild celebrations – including a new sword belt for William Wallace. After the battle Wallace was knighted, probably by Robert the Bruce himself, and was declared guardian of Scotland and leader of its armies.

THE BATTLE OF FALKIRK

In the aftermath of the battle Wallace raided Northumberland and Cumberland – Scotland was almost entirely clear of English forces at this point. Yet in the following summer Edward I invaded and defeated Wallace at the Battle of Falkirk on 22 July 1298, when the English king's cavalry and archers were far too much for Wallace's spearmen. One account of the battle reports that after the defeat, in flight from the battlefield, Wallace gained some consolation by overcoming and killing the

▲ *A highly idealized and sentimental Victorian view of the trial of William Wallace at Westminster.*

English knight Sir Brian de Jay, who was master of the English Templars. However, Wallace's reputation was ruined by the defeat and shortly afterwards he resigned as guardian of Scotland.

ESCAPE TO FRANCE?

Wallace disappeared from public view until his capture near Glasgow by the English on 5 August 1305. He may have carried on the battle against the English as a guerrilla fighter. According to tradition, however, he escaped to France – reputedly

▼ This 67m (220ft) sandstone Victorian Gothic monument near Stirling celebrates the career of Sir William Wallace and in particular his victory at Stirling Bridge.

he hid in the hold of a ship belonging to the pirate Richard Longoville, who was known as the 'Red Reiver' because of the red sails on his ships. Once at sea, Wallace was said to have burst from the hold, overpowered Longoville and forced him to carry Wallace and his men to France. He was also said to have travelled to Rome to ask the pope for aid against the English.

A TERRIBLE DEATH

After his capture Wallace was taken to London, where he was tried for treason – reputedly wearing a garland of oak leaves to signify that he was 'king of the outlaws'. He denied that he could have committed treason since he did not accept Edward I as his king, and was loyal only to King John Balliol of Scotland. After the trial, which inevitably found him guilty, Wallace was stripped naked and dragged by his heels through London to Smithfield, where he was hanged, drawn and quartered. His severed head was displayed on London Bridge and the four parts of his body put up in Aberdeen, Berwick, Newcastle and Stirling.

DEFENDER OF FRENCH CHIVALRY

MARSHAL DE BOUCICAUT

Jean le Meingre, known as Boucicaut, was a leading French knight of the 14th and 15th centuries, a major figure of the Hundred Years War, who also fought on crusades against the pagan Lithuanians in Prussia and against the Moors in Spain. He was famed for his skill in the saddle and defeated many of the greatest English knights of the day in the lists during the celebrated Jousts of St Inglevert in 1390. He also founded a chivalric order devoted to maintaining and defending the ideals of courtly love.

Boucicaut's feats were celebrated in a biography *Le livre des faits du Jean le Meingre, dit Boucicaut (An account of the deeds of Jean le Meingre, also known as Boucicaut)*. The romanticized account combined real events with conventional stages in the life of a hero. It was written in 1408, while its subject was still alive, indicating the status he had achieved as an exemplar of chivalry.

▲ *Marshal de Boucicaut's final acts of chivalry were performed on the battlefield at Agincourt on 25 October 1415. He spent his last years as an English prisoner.*

LIFE AS A SQUIRE AND FIRST MILITARY ENCOUNTERS

Boucicaut began his chivalric education as a page at the court of King Charles VI of France. He had his first taste of military action at the age of just 12, when he rode out on campaign in the company of Louis II, Duke of Bourbon, in Normandy. He was knighted by the duke at the age of 16 in November 1382 and the next day fought in the Battle of Roosebeke in the County of Flanders (now in Belgium). He distinguished himself as the Duke of Bourbon's army defeated a Flemish force led by Philip van Artevelde.

Boucicaut's romanticized biography states that he was well in advance of other young people in his skill at the chivalric pastimes, and that he grew up at a distance from others, with a natural reserve and haughtiness that his biographer deemed appropriate for a knight.

Two years later, in 1384, Boucicaut served alongside the knights of the Teutonic Order on their crusade against the pagan Lithuanians. Reputedly he was hungry to find opportunities to prove himself as a knight, and frustrated by a lack of warfare in France. Subsequently, he fought against the Moors in Spain, and afterwards travelled widely, as far as the Holy Land.

THE JOUSTS AT ST INGLEVERT

In 1390 Boucicaut and two other knights, Reginald de Roye and the Lord de Sempy, issued a challenge to fight all comers in a tournament at St Inglevert, near Boulogne, northern France. A year's truce was in place in the long war between England and France, and the challenge had the backing of King Charles VI of France, who made a grant of 6,000 francs to the defenders.

The French knights pledged that they would hold the lists for 30 days from 20 May. The challengers had to indicate on the day before they intended to fight whether they were to compete *à outrance* ('to the uttermost', with a sharpened lance) or *à plaisance* (in a joust of peace, 'for the pleasure', with a blunted lance). They were to do this by touching either a shield of war or a shield of peace put up by the defenders on a spruce tree beside the lists and giving their name, country and the name of their family to the nearby herald. Letters publicizing the challenge were sent far and wide, and as many as 100 knights and squires came from England, with around 40 from other countries.

There were 39 jousts in all, held on the 21–24 May, most fought *à outrance* but none resulting in death or serious injuries. The chronicle report of the event said that the jousting was of a very high standard, with several knights being knocked from their horses, many more losing helmets,

▼ *Boucicaut was a loyal servant of his country and the French king Charles VI, seen here at court receiving English envoys.*

and a large number of lances broken. King Charles VI reportedly attended the event incognito. There was no more jousting after 24 May although the three French knights 'held the lists' as promised in their challenge until 20 June. They were afterwards received as heroes in France.

MARSHAL OF FRANCE

On Christmas Day 1391, principally because of his great service as a crusader against heathens in Prussia and Livonia, Boucicaut was made Marshal of France by King Charles VI in a ceremony at the Cathedral of St Martin in Tours. In 1396 Boucicaut then took part in the Crusade of Nicopolis, as part of an army from France, the Holy Roman Empire, Hungary, Poland, England and other countries against the Ottoman Empire. This campaign ended in a major defeat at the Battle of Nicopolis in which the French general Jean de Vienne was killed and several knights, including Boucicaut, were taken prisoner. He was later ransomed.

THE ENTERPRISE OF THE GREEN SHIELD OF THE WHITE LADY

Back in Europe, in 1399 Boucicaut founded the chivalric order of the *Emprise de l'Escu Vert à la Dame Blanche*

▲ *Boucicaut was one of the three illustrious French knights who jousted against all challengers at St Inglevert in May 1390.*

('Enterprise of the Green Shield of the White Lady'). It had 12 knights as members, sworn for a period of five years to protect women who suffered oppression, particularly widows. Like the other main chivalric orders, the Green Shield of the White Lady had strong associations with tourneying – the order's members pledged to provide opponents in the lists for those who were required by a vow to a lady to perform a specific deed in a tournament but who could not find any competitors.

In 1401 King Charles VI appointed Boucicaut as the governor of Genoa, which had come under French control in 1396. Boucicaut had some success in conflicts against Venice and Cyprus, but the appointment proved short-lived, for the Genoese rid themselves of French control in 1409, while Boucicaut himself was absent on other business.

DEFEAT AT AGINCOURT

Boucicaut fought in the Battle of Agincourt in 1415, where he commanded the French vanguard. Following the English victory he was taken prisoner, and he died in Yorkshire in 1421 after spending his final years in captivity. His body was returned to France and buried in Tours.

THE EAGLE OF BRITTANY

BERTRAND DU GUESCLIN

Breton knight Bertrand du Guesclin, one of the great war captains of his age and a principal commander on the French side in the Hundred Years War, was another warrior celebrated in near-contemporary chivalric biographies. Known as a skilled general, who used guerrilla tactics to great effect against the English army, du Guesclin was famed above all for his impressive feats of arms. He was hailed as 'the Eagle of Brittany'.

Du Guesclin achieved legendary status in his lifetime, and was celebrated shortly after his death in 1380 in the *Chronique de Bertrand du Guesclin* (*Chronicle of Bertrand du Guesclin*), a poem written by Cuvelier. He rose from relatively humble origins among the minor nobility of Brittany to become the Constable of France between 1370 and 1380, and the biographical poem emphasized the point that through deeds of arms it was feasible for squires to attain greatness from humble beginnings.

POOR PROSPECTS

Cuvelier's account emphasized that early in life the future knight's prospects looked poor. His parents were put off by his unattractive, swarthy looks and his aggressive manner, and although he was their eldest son (of ten children) they treated him like a mere servant. However, a passing nun predicted great things for the young man and caused the parents to think again. Then he ran away from home and lived for a while as a leader of warring gangs of village boys.

THE UNKNOWN KNIGHT

We know little of du Guesclin's early career. Cuvelier made up a story that he distinguished himself, aged 17, as an

▲ *Bertrand du Guesclin rose to high office, but was renowned for his simple warrior qualities – generosity and great energy.*

unknown knight at a tournament in 1337 at Rennes. The story recounted how du Guesclin arrived on a carthorse at the tournament, at which his father was competing. With such inadequate equipment, the young man was laughed out of the lists, but he managed to borrow armour and a horse from one of his cousins. He entered the tournament lists with the visor of his helmet closed, so that no one could recognize him, and defeated 12 knights, knocking every one of them from their horses. When his own father challenged him (not knowing who he was) du Guesclin refused to fight. He then jousted on until a Norman knight rode up to him and raised his visor with the tip of his lance: all were astounded at the disclosure, and his father was delighted to see the young man's true identity.

In the 1340s du Guesclin appears to have fought as a 'robber knight' from a base in Paimpont forest, near Rennes,

▼ *Du Guesclin's chivalric qualities earned him his elevation to the rarefied position of Constable of France by Charles V in 1370.*

harassing English forces. One story recounted how he took the castle of Grand Fougeray with a clever ruse: he disguised some of his companions as woodcutters, and sent them to the castle gates carrying stacks of wood. The English garrison let them in, then the 'woodcutters' flung down their wood and so blocked the gates open, allowing support troops to enter and take the castle.

KNIGHTING AND EARLY SUCCESSES

In fact du Guesclin was not a squire who leaped to glory – he was already 34 years old when he was knighted on the battle-field while serving under Marshal Arnoul d'Audrehem. He received the honour after distinguishing himself in a minor engage-ment in 1354 while repelling a raid by the English knight Sir Hugh Calveley. In 1356–57 he defended Rennes during a siege set by Henry of Grosmont, 1st Duke of Lancaster (one of the founder members of the Order of the Garter). Although du Guesclin was eventually forced to pay 100,000 crowns to the English army, the

▼ *It was a dark day for France when the 'Eagle of Brittany' succumbed to dysentery on campaign in the Languedoc. The castle that he captured in his last military action is visible in the background.*

▲ *Du Guesclin (left) lowers his lance to avoid fighting his father in the celebrated – and apocryphal – story of how he entered the lists as an unknown knight and defeated no fewer than 12 established knights.*

staunch resistance went a long way to restoring French spirits after the utter humiliation of the Battle of Poitiers.

In 1364 du Guesclin won a resounding victory over the army of King Charles II of Navarre at the Battle of Cocherel. The conflict was part of a disputed claim over the Duchy of Burgundy, and du Guesclin's triumph forced Charles II to abandon his claim to the duchy and make peace with King Charles V of France.

TWO DEFEATS, TWO RANSOMS

However, later that same year du Guesclin suffered a major defeat at the Battle of Auray, which was part of the Breton War of Succession between John de Montfort (supported by the English) and Charles de Blois (supported by the French). Du Guesclin was captured and subsequently ransomed for 40,000 gold francs by the king. Then in 1367 he was fighting in Spain in support of Henry of Trastamara against King Pedro of Castile when he was defeated by Edward the Black Prince in the Battle of Najera (Navarette) and again

captured. On this occasion du Guesclin was allowed to name his own ransom – and set a seemingly unpayable amount, reputedly 100,000 francs. Such was his reputation, and his value to the French cause, that the money was raised by the king and du Guesclin was returned to France.

COMMANDER OF FRANCE

The Hundred Years War against England was renewed in 1369 and du Guesclin retook Poitou and Saintonge from English control. He achieved his country's highest military honour when he was made Constable of France in 1370. He went on to regain large areas of France from the English during the 1370s, using the tactic of avoiding pitched battles until the French were in a sufficiently advantageous position to win.

Bertrand du Guesclin died in 1380 due to dysentery while on campaign in the Languedoc. His life ended, appropriately enough, in a military success – he had just taken the castle of Châteauneuf de Randon from its English garrison. Accounts of his death tell how the captain of the garrison brought the keys and laid them on du Guesclin's body. Such was his stature that he was buried in the tomb of the French kings in the Saint-Denis Basilica, Paris.

HERO IN THE LISTS

JACQUES DE LALAING

The 15th-century knight Jacques de Lalaing was one of the greatest tourneyers of his day. He achieved such renown during his life that he became the subject of two contemporary biographies: the *Chronique de Jacques de Lalaing* (*Chronicle of Jacques de Lalaing*) and the *Livre des faits de Jacques de Lalaing* (*Book Recording the Deeds of Jacques de Lalaing*).

Jacques was born to a noble family from Wallonia (Belgium), and received his chivalric education as an associate of the Duke of Cleves at the court of Burgundy. He won notice in his teens and early 20s in the tiltyard. In 1443, according to the biographies, he excelled during a daring raid carried out by the Duke of Burgundy on the city of Luxembourg. The raiding party used ladders to scale the city walls at night and were at large in the streets before dawn. The city's residents burst from their houses fully armed and heavily armoured but Jacques accomplished many astonishing feats of chivalry with sword and lance, which added to his reputation.

FAME AT NANCY

In 1445, the biographies continue, Jacques amazed onlookers with his performance in a tournament at Nancy held in the presence of the kings of France, Aragon and Sicily. He won four jousts on the first day, even beating an experienced knight from the Auvergne whom he hit so hard on the helmet with his lance that sparks flew and the knight was knocked unconscious.

Jacques was treated as a hero that night and received many gifts from admirers. On the next day he defeated no fewer than eight more knights, but through all this he showed humility and noble bearing.

It was the normal practice in these chivalrous biographies for chroniclers to praise the achievement of their subjects very highly, and exaggerate them, sometimes combining actual events from the life history with exemplary events from a

typical knight's life. However, in the case of Jacques de Lalaing, although many of the events described were extraordinary we know that they were true. The principal author of the *Livre des faits de Jacques de Lalaing* was Jean le Fèvre de St Remy, who served as herald to the Order of the Golden Fleece. His balanced account of Jacques's life does not gloss over the times when the knight almost met his match.

'FEATS OF ARMS'

In the same year, 1445, Jacques embarked upon his 'feats of arms' – prearranged encounters with other knights fought in full armour with weapons of war but according to agreed rules – either a fixed

▲ *In the tournament at Nancy, Jacques struck one opponent from his saddle so hard that he landed a full 7m (24ft) away.*

number of courses on horseback and on foot, or until one of the combatants was knocked to the ground. The first meeting was in Antwerp with Jean de Boniface, an Italian knight who was on a tour seeking opportunities to prove his chivalric worth. The agreed terms were for jousting until one of the knights broke six lances, then fighting on foot using first spears, then poleaxes, swords or daggers. The fight would end when one knight surrendered, or touched the ground with his hand, knee or any part of his body.

Before the contest commenced, Jacques was knighted by the Duke of Burgundy. As was appropriate Jacques then proved himself worthy of the honour: he disarmed de Boniface by knocking the poleaxe out of his hands, then forced him backwards with his own weapon. The Duke of Burgundy, who was refereeing, brought the contest to an end.

IN CASTILE AND SCOTLAND

In 1446–47 Jacques went on tour seeking glory, in the course of which he defeated a champion in Castile. In 1449 with his uncle Simon de Lalaing and a Breton squire named Herve de Meriadec, Jacques fought in a 'combat of six' against three Scottish knights at Stirling, before the king of Scotland. In fierce combat Jacques and his compatriots acquitted themselves well.

Later that year in Bruges he defeated an English squire, Thomas Que, when he came as close to defeat as he ever would after his hand was badly cut by the spike of the English squire's poleaxe. Yet, in great pain and with blood flowing, Jacques fought on and threw Que to the ground.

▼ *In a long career in the lists Jacques saw off many challengers, but neither he or nor any knight could withstand siege cannon, one of which ended his life at Poucques.*

▲ *In many of Jacques's 'feats of arms', jousting was followed by fighting on foot.*

'PASSAGE OF THE FOUNTAIN OF WEEPING'

Jacques then announced a challenge to all-comers to defeat him in a passage of arms. He was to erect a pavilion on the first day of every month from 1 November 1449 to 30 September 1450 and accept challenges to fight, either on horseback with lances, or on foot, either with poleaxes or with swords. The pavilion was hung with three shields, representing the three types of combat: challengers approached the pavilion and touched the appropriate shield. It was next to a fountain with a statue of a weeping woman and Jacques's challenge was called the 'Passage of the Fountain of Weeping'. He remained undefeated throughout the entire year, fighting 11 knights and squires. He entered some of the conflicts without armour on his right leg, and in one he fought without an armoured gauntlet on his right hand.

Afterwards Jacques made a pilgrimage to Rome. When he returned to the court of Burgundy he received a hero's welcome. In 1451 he was admitted to the chivalric brotherhood of the Order of the Golden Fleece, founded by Philip the Good, Duke of Burgundy, in 1430.

Jacques was killed by cannon fire while fighting for the duke of Burgundy at the siege of Poucques on 3 July 1453 during a campaign against Ghent. Jacques was just 32 years old at the time of his death, which was given added poignancy by the sense that – as with 'the English Achilles', Sir John Talbot, killed by gunfire at Castillion just two weeks later on 17 July 1453 – modern weaponry had dispatched a great knight, one who understood the traditional ways of chivalry and fought according to them.

THE 'ENGLISH ACHILLES'

SIR JOHN TALBOT

John Talbot, 1st Earl of Shrewsbury, was probably the most daring English commander of the Hundred Years War, so feared by the French for the ferocity of his lightning campaigns in 1427–53 that he was called the 'English Achilles' in reference to the Greek warrior who vanquished Hector before the walls of Troy. Talbot was a prolific knight who won no fewer than 40 battles and minor encounters in France, where his speciality was in surprising the enemy and conducting very aggressive attacks. In a manner typical of the age in which he lived, he combined ruthlessness on the battlefield, and a liking for making trouble off it, with a deep respect for the chivalric tradition and a staunch Christian faith.

NO LOVER OF PEACE

Sir John was a soldier from his youth, and according to some accounts fought aged around 16 in the royal army at the Battle

▼ *King Henry VI of England, proclaimed as King of France following the death of the French king, Charles VI, invests Sir John Talbot as Constable of France in 1436.*

SIR JOHN TALBOT

Born: 1384

Died: 17 July 1453

Knighted: unknown; made a Knight of the Order of the Garter *c.*1424

Famous for: the ferocity and speed of attacks on French campaigns

Greatest achievement: routing the French forces at Ry, 1436 – despite commanding a far inferior force

---

of Shrewsbury in 1403 between King Henry IV of England and a rebel force under 'Hotspur' – Sir Henry Percy. Certainly by the following year he was serving the king in the wars against Welsh rebels, and he fought in Wales for five years until 1409.

In 1414–19 Talbot was Lieutenant of Ireland, and by this stage had already gained a reputation for ferocious raiding tactics, which he used against Gaelic chieftains. One local chronicler noted of him that 'from the time of King Herod there has never been a more wicked soldier here'. In Ireland and back in England he

was a troublemaker, quarrelling fiercely with rival lords, and at one stage being thrown into the Tower of London.

KNIGHT OF THE GARTER

Talbot served Henry V briefly in France then after the king's death in 1422 was made a Knight of the Garter in 1424 by Henry VI. In 1427 he began a long period of military service in France, during which he truly made his name.

But his start was not propitious: in 1428–29 he took part in the siege of Orléans, and was unable to prevent its relief by Joan of Arc, then in June 1429 he was captured at Patay and held in prison for four years. He was released only after the French knight keeping him captive was himself captured by the English.

FAMOUS VICTORIES IN FRANCE

Thereafter Talbot went from strength to strength. In 1434–35 he defended Paris against the French army, then in autumn 1435 he withdrew to Rouen to defend Normandy. Probably his most famous hour came in January 1436 when, with only a small force at his disposal and with Rouen under threat, he launched a surprise attack that completely wrong-footed a much larger French army at Ry. In 1436 he was appointed Constable of France. Another of his celebrated feats was the retaking of Pontoise in February 1437 when his army attacked across the winter ice at dawn on Ash Wednesday, and totally surprised a garrison that was still in recovery after the celebrations of Shrove Tuesday (Mardi Gras).

In 1439 Talbot won another victory with a small force against a 6,000-strong army under Constable Richemont. His swift manoeuvres were often an attempt to bring the enemy to battle. In 1441, for example, he chased a French army back and forth four times across the rivers Oise and Seine trying to force a pitched battle.

LAST OF THE GREAT KNIGHTS?

The way in which he met his end on 17 July 1453 enhanced his reputation. He was leading an attempt to relieve the town of Castillion, which was under French siege, and in characteristic fashion attempted to catch the French off guard with a swift attack. However, the French army was entrenched in a strong defensive position and had substantial artillery at its disposal. The English attack came to nothing and Talbot was shot when he attempted to rally his men. He was celebrated thereafter as one of a dying breed of great knights, and his death seemed to symbolize the collision between an old way of making war and the sheer destructive force of artillery guns.

For all that he was a troublesome man and could be utterly ruthless, Talbot had many notable chivalric qualities. Throughout his long career he was extremely loyal to the royal house of Lancaster, and as a military general he was admired for his spirited raiding and his bravery in battle. He had a genuine inter-

▼ The adventures imagined for questing knights could be quite exotic. In an image from a 'book of romances' given to Sir John by Margaret of Anjou c.1445, knights encounter some rather puny elephants.

est in the traditions of chivalry, and he compiled a collection of poems and handbooks that he gave to Margaret of Anjou when she married King Henry VI of England in 1445. He was a Knight of the Garter from 1424 to 1445, and quarrelled with fellow knight Sir John Falstoff whom

▲ Talbot died at Castillon in 1453. The attack he launched there, in the face of the French artillery, was rash – and resulted in his death. Following this defeat England lost nearly all its French possessions.

he accused of having disgraced the order when he fled from the field of battle at Patay. Talbot established a collection of ornaments with Garter decorations for use on St George's Day at the Church of the Sepulchre in Rouen. He went on pilgrimage to Rome in 1450.

Initially Talbot was buried at Castillion, where the French expressed their admiration for his chivalric life by building a chapel in his honour. (It was destroyed during the French Revolution, but a memorial continues to mark the place where he died.) On his death a French chronicler hailed him as one who had been a thorn in the side of the French for many years. Sir John had an enduring reputation for chivalry in England and is a significant character in Shakespeare's play *King Henry VI Part 2* (c.1590–91).

LOVERS, SAINTS AND OUTLAWS

Andreas Capellanus attempted to codify the rules of engagement between knights and their ladies at court in *De Amore* (*About Love* or *The Art of Courtly Love*), written in *c*.1190. Andreas argued that true love must be secret, difficult if not impossible to act on, and unconsummated. In this form it ennobled both the lover and the beloved and inspired the lover to great deeds of chivalry. The rarefied society of the knights and ladies who accepted the conventions of courtly love was at odds with the simple military ethos of the knights of Charlemagne who expressed themselves primarily through physical deeds, religious ardour and plain emotions. The primary concerns for those committed to courtly love were affairs of the heart and distinctions of status.

In much the same way the ideal of knighthood as represented in the image of the *miles Christi*, soldier of Christ, called for a saintly devotion to duty in protecting and defending the weak. The ideal found expression in the rule of life proposed for members of religious brotherhoods such as the Knights Templar, which called for poverty and chastity, as well in the chivalric literature in the figure of Sir Galahad, the purest of King Arthur's knights. Yet many knights did not live up to the ideal, and chivalric legends and romance also celebrated knights such as Robert le Diable, Guy of Warwick or Fulk Fitzwarin who fought from beyond the law, but were praised for their martial prowess and energy alongside the perfection of chivalry expressed in warrior saints such as St George.

▲ *Crusader knights fight in a battle.*

◄ *Medieval Christians interpreted the story of St George slaying the dragon as the victory of Christian chivalry over bestial sin and false religions.*

GAMES OF LOVE

HOW KNIGHTS PROVED THEIR DEVOTION

The interactions between ladies and their knights, in gardens or at tournaments, or even when knights departed on quests to prove their love, often resembled games. They were played for a high stake – the lady's love.

The 13th-century French poet and author of romances Jean Renart produced a striking vignette of highly refined courtly love in his narrative poem *Le Lai de l'Ombre* (*The Lay of the Shadow*) in *c.*1220. The poem concerns an educated knight, skilful in chivalric pastimes such as chess and hawking, who courted a married lady.

▼ *Jean de Saintré kneels before the lady, the Dame de Belles-Cousines, who is giving him an education in courtly love. Jean is a fictional knight, hero of a book (c.1450) by the Provençal author Antoine de la Sale.*

In the manner of courtly love, he had been captivated by her beauty from afar, and having been struck by love, he could apply himself to nothing, and dreamt longingly of his lady.

The poem presented the encounter between the two lovers almost like a chess match, with each attempting to outwit the other within the rules of the game of love, exhibiting detachment from their feelings. The knight approached his lady in a garden by a well, determined to win her over, and she welcomed him. Her first counter-argument to his statement of love was two-pronged: since he was courteous it was impossible that he should be without a true love already, and because he was so skilful in love he was no doubt an old hand at deluding ladies with stories of false devotion. He replied by saying that

her welcome showed that she was pleased to see him, but she responded that her friendliness was only social politeness.

She criticized him for being like many knights in misinterpreting social politeness as the sign of passion. He should not have aimed so high as to attempt to win her, she said. In reply he likened himself to Sir Tristan, describing how that knight had set sail without a mast, trusting in good fortune to bring him to Iseult. She replied and pointed out that she had a husband already who was a paragon of gallantry and chivalry.

The knight said that he was plunged in suffering and implied that it was her Christian duty to relieve it, likening her relieving his pangs of love to going on a crusade. He said he was ready to die for love of her. This gambit seemed to plunge her into deep thought.

Then he slipped a ring from her finger and put his own ring in its place, before quickly departing. Noticing too late what he had done, she recalled him. She said to him that if he loved her he would take it back because all lovers were bound by convention to do their lady's bidding. At this point it seemed that she had caught him. Then he looked down to where her face was reflected in the waters of the well and said he would give the ring to the one person he loved best after his lady; he then cast it on to her reflection saying that since she would not accept his gift or his love he would give it to her shadow. She was charmed by the courtesy of this gesture and accepted his offer of love.

COURTS OF LOVE

The intricate arguments in *Le Lai de l'Ombre* suggested that a third party might sometimes have been needed to judge the victor in the games of courtly love. Indeed, Andreas Capellanus's *De Amore* contained a number of judgements passed by great ladies on lovers at 'courts of love'. These

▲ *Skilful chess playing was one of the prescribed qualities of an educated knight who would make a suitable courtly suitor.*

courts were, in theory, like courts of law, but with ladies as their judges making their decisions according to the rules of courtly love.

The ladies mentioned by Andreas as judges included Eleanor of Aquitaine, Marie de Champagne and Ermengarde, Viscountess of Narbonne. In the 19th century, when the term 'courtly love' was first used, historians suggested that these courts of love actually sat and handed down judgements, but modern historians have been unable to find evidence that the courts existed beyond the references to them in poems. The latest thinking is that the courts mentioned in the poems were a poetic image for the meetings held by ladies, knights and poets at which they enjoyed poetry and debated the niceties of courtly love.

WILLIAM IX OF AQUITAINE

Troubadour poet William of Aquitaine was a man of extremely colourful character and behaviour who was twice excommunicated, yet he was also one of the leaders of the crusade of 1101. Duke of Aquitaine and Gascony, and Count of Poitou, William was the first known troubadour poet, writing poems concerned with love in the vernacular Provençal language. Eleven of his poems survive under the name Count of Poitou. He was outspoken, and happy to court controversy. One of his poems described a convent in which the nuns should be selected for their beauty – or their ability as whores.

The first time he was excommunicated, for failure to pay Church taxes, he confronted the bishop of Poitiers at sword point, but did not persuade him to withdraw the anathema. The second time he was excommunicated was for kidnapping the Viscountess Dangereuse, the wife of his vassal Aimery I of Rochefoucauld (although she appeared to have been willingly taken). William installed her in his castle despite the fact that he was himself married. His wife retired to a monastery at Fontevrault, and the viscountess lived openly with William – he even carried her image on his shield.

As a knight he was less than exemplary: he was reckless in battle and lost many encounters while on the 1101 crusade. He subsequently fought in Spain, again without much success. His enduring fame rests more on his poetry and on the influence he had over his granddaughter, Eleanor of Aquitaine, who became one of the great courtly patrons.

▼ *In the 13th-century French poem of courtly love, the* Roman de la Rose (Romance of the Rose)*, the garden is the arena for romance. The poem was composed in two halves: the first, by Guillaume de Lorris in c.1230; and the second, by Jean de Meung, in c.1280.*

IN A LADY'S SERVICE

A KNIGHT'S DUTIES IN LOVE

Knights believed that the love they felt for a lady was a spur to acts of great chivalry. As love of Christ and faith in God had driven knights of the First Crusade to overcome seemingly impossible odds and regain possession of Jerusalem, so more secular-minded chivalric successors from the mid-12th century onwards drew inspiration from the lady they admired at court.

A SPUR TO ACTS OF DARING

In c.1130 in his *History of the Kings of Britain*, Geoffrey of Monmouth noted during a description of a bohort or peaceful tournament held at the court of King Arthur, that 'the ladies refused to grant their love to any warlike man who had not proven his bravery three times in battle'. He added that, as a result, in order to win the love of fair ladies the knights of the Round Table were 'ever more daring'.

LADY BECOMES LORD

French troubadour Bernart de Ventadorn (c.1130–90) compared the ties between a lover and his lady to those of the feudal relationship between a knight and his suzerain (feudal superior). This became a common image in the poems of courtly love. As the knight conventionally went through a long training, first as page, then as squire and finally as knight, so a lover would have to emerge from the ranks of hopeful admirers to be accepted as a devoted suitor and, in cases of high achievement, might finally become the lady's lover.

The knight offered service to the lady, as in a feudal relationship, and she offered protection to the knight, just as a feudal lord would. From this idea developed the custom of knights wearing a lady's 'favour' – usually a scarf or cloth – in tournaments or during a campaign. From the lady's love, or at least her interest, the knight drew strength.

To win the love of his lady the knight had to impress her. All his chivalric traits – bravery, courtesy, generosity, prowess and loyalty – were used to this end in order to generate his worth in her eyes.

A DISTANT TARGET

Within the conventions of courtly love some knights declared their love for and devotion to ladies they had not even met. Just hearing tales of a lady's beauty and the perfection of her bearing and manners was enough in some cases to convince a knight to dedicate himself to her service. Even if she were close at hand, the lady was often elevated far above the knight who devoted himself to her. She could prove a very hard mistress to please – in many cases the greatest deeds of devotion were not enough to win her favour.

OBEDIENCE EVEN UNTO SHAME

The knight had also to be obedient to his lady. In chivalric literature knights were sometimes ordered by their lady to do

◀ *For honour, and to win the admiration of his lady, a knight throws himself lustily into the jousting at a country* pas d'armes.

what must almost have been unthinkable – to fight deliberately badly at tournaments and bring shame on themselves. In the Old French romance *Perlesvaus* (*c*.1210) Sir Gawain was told by his lady to identify himself among the other identically armoured knights in the lists by losing repeatedly. He was obedient. When a knight approached to fight, Gawain fled on horseback and spent the rest of the tournament hiding behind King Arthur. (In a colourful image the romance said that Gawain was clinging as closely to Arthur as a magpie clings to a bush when it is trying to escape falcons that are intent on seizing it.)

Gawain lost a great deal of honour in the escapade, for Arthur was greatly ashamed of his knight and the other knights commented openly that Gawain did not serve his great reputation. But he was sustained by the knowledge that he had done it out of motives of the purest chivalry – to prove that his love for his lady was stronger even than his concern for his standing at court.

JOURNEYS OF DEVOTION

It was a duty for newly made knights to seek opportunities to prove themselves worthy of their new condition. This was

▼ *As part of his adventures in Chrétien de Troyes's* Knight of the Cart, *Sir Lancelot beheads Sir Meleagant, who had abducted Guinevere, and presents the head to her.*

▲ *A devoted knight returns at the end of a quest in this romantic painting from 1921 by Sir Frank Bernard Dicksee.*

one reason why knights were often made at the start of a campaign or just prior to a battle, because the knighting was a spur to acts of chivalry. In the same way, within the conventions of courtly love, a knight who had just won a lady's attention or love was expected to find ways of proving himself worthy of her. This often involved embarking on a career of knight errantry, travelling away from the lady and seeking adventures to win her love.

THE CHURCH AND COURTLY LOVE

The Catholic Church condemned the conventions and culture of courtly love. The official Church position was that marriage was a sacrament of the Christian Church and that within it sex was acceptable only as a means of procreation – ideally, Christians of the period were expected to be celibate. The poets of courtly love, on the other hand, praised romantic love, often between knights and married ladies, emphasized the power of sexual attraction and implied that acts of adultery were understandable when passions ran so high. One response of the Church in the 12th century was to begin to promote the cult of the Virgin Mary, Mother of Christ, as a focus for some of the passionate devotion that was otherwise directed along secular channels in love affairs and courtly love attachments.

KNIGHTS ERRANT
TOURS OF CHIVALRY

A familiar figure in the medieval romances, a knight errant was a knight who embarked on a long journey of adventures, often to prove his worth to his chosen lady, in order to win or justify her love. The journey generally involved marvellous adventures such as encounters with giants or rogue knights.

THE FIRST KNIGHT ERRANT
The first knight known as a knight errant in chivalric literature was Sir Gawain in the late 14th-century English poem *Sir Gawain and the Green Knight*. Challenged to attend the Green Knight's chapel after a year had passed, Sir Gawain embarked on a long journey with many adventures. When he reached the castle of Sir Bercilak (who turned out to be the Green Knight), he was greeted as a 'knyght erraunt'.

▼ *The slaying of a dragon was one among the many feats of strength performed by Sir Yvain, with his companion the Lion.*

However, many knights undertook a life of adventures of the kind we now call 'knight errantry' long before the Gawain poem was written. The convention had its roots both in the extravagant adventures of folklore – such as the Welsh legends which contain the earliest accounts of Arthurian knights – and in the tourneying trips embarked upon by knights as early as the 11th or 12th centuries. On these tours knights would travel to different tournaments seeking sport, renown and wealth through taking ransoms.

A FRANKISH KNIGHT AT THE CROSSROADS
An anecdote told of a Frankish knight during the First Crusade indicates that when knights embarked upon these trips seeking adventures they expected contests on their travels as well as at more formal tournaments. The story, told by Anna Comnena, daughter of Byzantine emperor Alexius Comnenus, tells of a Frankish

▲ *A lady attends to her knight as he prepares to embark on the quest to which she has commanded him.*

knight who sat on the imperial throne of Byzantium in the presence of her father, and was reprimanded for his lack of respect. He responded with defiant pride, declaring himself a noble Frank, saying that back in the French countryside there was a well-known place for issuing and answering challenges to combat to prove one's worth as a knight. The spot was at a crossroads near an old shrine and any knight could wait there, ready to fight, until another warrior came who was brave enough to compete and determine who was the most chivalrous. The knight in Anna Comnena's story said he was so famous that, although he had often waited there, no one had ever challenged him.

THE KNIGHT WITH THE LION
For some knights the voyage as a knight errant became an end in itself, and undermined the relationship with the lady. The Arthurian knight Sir Yvain, for example,

stayed away so long on his journey of adventures that he clean forgot his lady at court – his wife, Lady Laudine – and for a while she banned him from returning.

Sir Yvain was based on Owain, an Arthurian knight in Welsh legend, where he was married to the sister of Iseult and in some versions was said to be the son of a goddess named Modron (a version of the witch Morgan le Fay). His story was given prominence by French poet Chrétien de Troyes in his poem *Yvain, the Knight of the Lion* (*c.*1170). In this account, Sir Yvain travelled into a magical forest to challenge a knight called Sir Esclados, who had defeated and humiliated Yvain's cousin, Sir Calogrenant. Sir Yvain killed Sir Esclados, then won the love of his widow, Lady Laudine, whom he married.

Back at court, Sir Gawain persuaded Sir Yvain to embark on a voyage of adventures and Lady Laudine allowed him to go on condition that he return within a year. When he forgot about her and she banned him from returning, Sir Yvain went mad with grief but at last recovered sufficiently to attempt to win her love back. He saved a lion from a serpent, and it became his companion, travelling with him as a symbol of his chivalric virtue: he became known as the 'Knight of the Lion'. Finally, impressed by his achievement, Lady Laudine permitted Sir Yvain to return.

As we saw in Chapter Five, this story was used as the basis for the staging of an Arthurian tournament held at Le Hem, Picardy, in 1278 by the lords of Bazentin and Longueval, when Robert II, Count of Artois, appeared as Sir Yvain with a live lion in his company. The stories of knight errantry were frequently the inspiration for theatrical enactments at tournaments, and there were many other examples of travelling knights in the Arthurian tales, notably in the story of Sir Lancelot.

SIR AMADIS OF GAUL

Another celebrated knight errant in the Arthurian tradition was the Portuguese hero Sir Amadis of Gaul, whose tale of wandering adventures dated from the

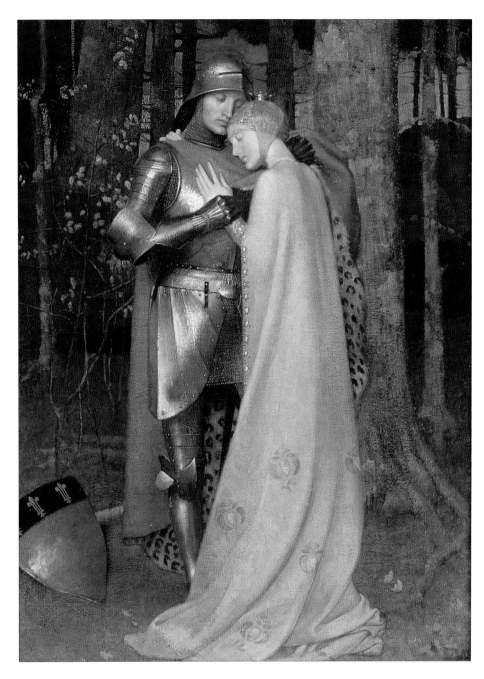

early 14th century. It was published in 1508 and became a great bestseller in Spain and Portugal in the 16th century.

Sir Amadis was said to be the son of Queen Elisena of England and King Períon of Gaul, and was abandoned on a barge in England. He had a chivalric upbringing from a knight named Sir Gandales in Scotland, then was knighted by King Períon and went through many adventures in an enchanted land. His lady, Oriana, became jealous of him and sent a letter denouncing him, which plunged him into madness from which he recovered only when Oriana's maid was sent to save him.

▲ *The forest – and in particular areas near water – was the haunt of female spirits. Warriors often encountered temptations of love on their trips of knight errantry.*

After fighting in support of Lady Oriana's father, King Lisuarte, he travelled for ten years as the 'Knight of the Green Sword' and ventured as far away as Constantinople where he defeated a great giant. Throughout his adventures Sir Amadis showed himself courteous and sensitive, and devoutly Christian, as well as unbeatable in battle and unafraid to spill blood.

THE GLORIES OF CHIVALRIC LOVE

ULRICH VON LICHTENSTEIN, JAUFRÉ RUDEL, LORD OF BLAYE AND SIR WILLIAM MARMION

The knights errant described in courtly romances had many imitators in the medieval era. The 13th-century Austrian knight and Minnesänger Ulrich von Lichtenstein described how he embarked on a long journey of adventure and fought in many tournaments to prove his love to his lady. The reputed feats of 12th-century French knight and troubadour Jaufré Rudel, Lord of Blaye, and those of the 14th-century English knight Sir William Marmion make intriguing comparisons.

JOURNEY IN A LADY'S SERVICE

Ulrich von Lichtenstein was a leading noble from the Duchy of Styria (now southern Austria), who served Margrave Heinrich of Istria as page and squire and was knighted in 1222 (in his early 20s) by Duke Leopold VI of Austria. He was also a notable poet, and portrayed himself as a chivalric knight and courtly lover par excellence in his 1255 poem *Frauendienst* (*Service of the Lady*).

According to the poem, Ulrich travelled from Venice to Vienna in 1226 disguised as the Roman goddess of love, Venus, to win honour for his lady. Every knight he met he challenged to a joust in his lady's name. In the course of his travels he broke no fewer than 307 lances and was undefeated in a single joust. But his lady remained unimpressed, and demanded further deeds to prove his devotion. He then planned a second quest in honour of a different lady, and disguised as King Arthur, but he never managed to embark on this quest.

In his poem he declared that a knight who, with courage in his heart, won the praise of his lady thereby also won great honour. He also declared that the knight should banish fear entirely, because the smallest trace of cowardice would make him unworthy of his lady's attentions, and he should also be willing to die rather than fail in order to win her acclaim.

JAUFRÉ RUDEL AND LOVE FROM AFAR

Jaufré Rudel, Lord of Blaye (near modern Bordeaux in western France), was a knight and troubadour of great renown in the mid-12th century about whom a colourful fictionalized biography was created.

In his poems he specialized in the convention of knights loving from afar ladies they may never have met. One of the few references to him outside his surviving songs – in a poem by the 12th-century troubadour Marcabru – suggests that he was *oltra mar* ('beyond the sea' – that is, on crusade). Rudel probably died while travelling on the Second Crusade, which took place between 1145 and 1149.

The legend of his life told that he took the cross and went on crusade because he was inflamed with a desire to glimpse and honour Countess Hodierna of Tripoli, whose beauty and dignity were praised lavishly by travel-weary pilgrims coming back from the Holy Land. He declared her to be his *amour de loin* ('distant love') and pledged his devotion to her before he departed; but during the voyage he fell terribly ill and when he reached Tripoli he was close to death. The countess, hearing of his devotion and his serious illness, descended from her castle to see him, and held the knight in her arms. In that instant he died in an ecstasy of fulfilled desire blended with a deep sense of his own unworthiness.

◀ *Knights could not really have jousted in the rounded area represented in this illustration from the 15th century. The knight on the left wears a fine heraldic swan on the top of his helmet.*

THE EXAMPLE OF SIR WILLIAM MARMION

In the 14th-century border wars fought between England and Scotland, Sir William Marmion rode to almost certain death to satisfy his lady's desire for renown. In *c*.1320 the Scots had the upper hand in the border conflict, and the castle of Norham in Northumberland was the scene of almost constant fighting between its English garrison and Scottish raiders. Around this time Sir William Marmion was feasting at Lincoln when his lady sent him a gilt-crested war helmet with the message that he should seek out the most dangerous place in the land to win her acclaim by wearing it in battle. He took counsel with his fellow knights at the feast and all agreed the best place to go would be Norham, so he travelled there with the splendid helmet in his possession.

Only four days after his arrival, a great raiding party numbering 160 brave-hearted warriors marched to the castle. The castle constable, Sir Thomas de Gray, called on Sir William and persuaded him that this was his chance to attain glory: 'Sir knight,' he declared, 'you have come to make your helmet famous … Climb on your horse, behold your enemies, use your glittering spurs to launch a charge into their midst.' The constable said that he would prepare to fight but would hold back until Sir William had had his chance to prove his worth.

▼ *By 1823, when JMW Turner painted this view of Norham Castle in Northumberland, the scene of Sir William Marmion's heroics was a romantic ruin.*

▲ *A knight takes leave of his noble wife. His exploits on campaign or his adventures win honour both for himself and for his lady.*

Then, wearing magnificent armour that shone with gold and silver, and with his bright helmet sparkling in the sunlight, Sir William rode out alone to take on the raiders. He put up a noble fight, but was so outnumbered that he was injured in the face, dragged from his horse and was at risk of death. At this point Sir Thomas and the knights of the garrison rode out and drove all the raiders back in disarray; they helped Sir William remount and at his side they chased the raiders far into the countryside. William Marmion's chivalric feat is told in the chronicle *Scalacronica* written in *c*.1355 by Sir Thomas Gray, son of the Sir Thomas in the narrative.

ORLANDO IN LOVE
THE ROMANCES OF ITALY

A new cycle of romance epics in 15th- and 16th-century Italy cast a fresh light on the adventures of Roland, Oliver and other paragons of chivalry at the court of Charlemagne. Matteo Maria Boiardo's poem *Orlando Innamorato* (*Orlando in Love*) and Lodovico Ariosto's *Orlando Furioso* (*Orlando Maddened*) combined the military feats of Charlemagne's knights with narratives of courtly love that were developed in the Arthurian romances.

LOVE SEEN THROUGH A KNIGHT'S EYES
Matteo Maria Boiardo was a knight and a lyric poet. He served as captain of Modena in 1480–82 and of Reggio in 1487–94. He wrote a highly personal collection of love poems, describing his passion for Antonia Caprara and published in 1499 as *Amorum libri tres* (*Three Books on Love*). His

▼ *Orlando learns the terrible news that Angelica has eloped with the Saracen knight Medoro to Cathay (China). The scene is from Lodovico Ariosto's* Orlando Furioso.

Orlando Innamorato was the first poem to combine elements from the Carolingian and Arthurian romances. Boiardo also added classical influences, for he was a poet during the Italian Renaissance and translated many classical works by authors including Herodotus, Xenophon and Apuleius.

Boiardo's epic, which was left unfinished at his death, described the quests of Orlando (Roland) and many other knights to win the love of the beautiful pagan princess Angelica, daughter of Galafrone, the king of Cathay (China), and her love for Orlando's cousin Ranaldo. (Ranaldo was previously encountered in the *Doon de Mayence* cycle of *chansons de geste* as the hero Renaud de Montauban.) These quests, which included a full complement of bruising encounters, amid celebrations of great icons of the chivalric tradition such as the horse Bayard, with magical spells and exotic characters, were set against the background of Charlemagne in Paris coming under attack from a great Moorish army. In *Orlando Innamorato* the

virtues of religious faith, military honour and love of one's country are celebrated above all others.

LOVESTRUCK AT THE TOURNAMENT
Orlando Innamorato began with an account of a great tournament held in Paris by Charlemagne. The beautiful Angelica and her brother and champion Argalia arrived, declaring that whoever could defeat Argalia could have the hand in marriage of Angelica.

Orlando fell in love with Angelica at first sight, despite the fact that the beautiful Lady Alda (in this version of events, his wife) was at his side. Argalia proved to be invincible since he wore magic armour; he and his sister had really come to lay low the great champions of Charlemagne in preparation for an invasion by an army of Moors led by Agramante, Emperor of Africa. Argalia was also drawn by the fame of the Frankish knights: he wanted above all to capture Orlando's famous sword (here known as Durindan) and Ranaldo's horse Bayard.

After the first two jousts, in which Argalia triumphed, he and Angelica withdrew into a magical forest called the Forest of Arden. The leading knights of the court followed. Ranaldo drank from a magical stream whose waters made a knight hate his lady: thereafter he loathed Angelica. She, on the other hand, drank water from a stream that made those who did so fall in love, and seeing Ranaldo asleep nearby she fell in love with him. He woke, saw her, looked on her with hatred and rode away. She fell asleep on the ground.

Orlando found Angelica and was watching her when he was challenged by a passing knight – a typical event in the romances and tales of knight errantry, and one that made them popular as themes for enactment at tournaments of the age of chivalry. The knight, named Feraguto,

▲ *Sir Roger, a knight in* Orlando Furioso, *rescues Lady Angelica while mounted on a hippogriff – a legendary creature that is half horse and half griffin.*

fought with Orlando until they were interrupted by Feraguto's sister Fiordespina, who told him he had to return to Spain to defend his homeland against attack by an Asian king.

FIGHT IN AN ENCHANTED GLADE

Many more adventures followed. Orlando spent a period in an enchanted garden where he forgot his love of Angelica, his loyalty to Charlemagne and even his own love of honour, but he escaped and then at Angelica's castle at Albraca (believed to be Bukhara in Uzbekistan) he fought a Tartar emperor, Agricane, who was

another rival for Angelica's love. Their epic battle, in a magical forest, went on all day and through the night by moonlight until dawn. When finally Orlando prevailed, his rival declared his desire to become a Christian and begged to be baptized. Orlando consented to his wish and baptized him at a fountain in the wood.

ORLANDO DRIVEN TO MADNESS

The wanderings of Ranaldo, Orlando and Angelica eventually led them back to France, where Charlemagne was still being besieged by a pagan army. The poem was left unfinished at Boiardo's death but a continuation was written by Lodovico Ariosto in his poem *Orlando Furioso*, published in 1516.

Ariosto was a knight and courtier who, after briefly serving as commander of the

citadel of Canossa, was in the service of Cardinal Ippolito d'Este and later became governor of the province of Garfagnana in the Apennines. His poem was also set against the backdrop of a war between Christians commanded by Charlemagne, and Saracens led by Agramante near Paris. Ariosto's poem described how Orlando was driven into madness and despair by his unrequited love for Angelica, while a pagan champion named Ruggiero (who was a descendant of the ancient paragon of chivalry, Hector of Troy) devoted himself to the Christian maiden Bradamante. She was Ranaldo's sister and rode in white armour as the 'Virgin Knight'. The plot involving them was a tribute to the poet's patrons, the Este family, who were traditionally said to be descended from these two lovers.

WHEN A CHRISTIAN LOVED A PAGAN

IF KNIGHTS OF ONE FAITH LOVED LADIES OF ANOTHER

Tales of love between Christians and pagans, such as that between the pagan warrior Ruggiero and the Christian maiden Bradamante in *Orlando Furioso*, were a common theme in the courtly romances. Another great Italian epic poem, *Jerusalem Delivered* by Torquato Tasso, cast the historical figure of Tancred de Hauteville, who was a hero of the First Crusade, as the central figure of a romance, and invented a love affair for him with a Muslim warrior maiden named Clorinda. Such difficult inter-faith romances allowed for enchanting adventures in exotic locations as well as celebration of the ultimate triumph of the 'true faith' – it was an essential conclusion, as in *Orlando Furioso*, for the pagan to renounce his or her faith and seek baptism in Christianity.

A TALE TOLD BY CRUSADERS

A very popular version of this narrative was *Floire et Blancheflor*, a 12th-century French metrical romance that told of the undying love between Floire, warrior son of a Saracen king, and Blancheflor, the daughter of a Christian countess. The story is believed to have come originally from a Greco-Byzantine source, and was perhaps brought back to Europe from the Holy Land by crusader knights returning from a campaign.

The oldest known version of the tale was a French one of *c.*1160, and after 1200 it appeared for about 150 years in a variety of vernacular versions across Europe. An English romance version, *Floris and Blanchefleur*, of *c.*1250, was extremely well received. In the 14th century Giovanni Boccaccio told a version of the same story in his *Decameron* (*c.*1350).

PILGRIMS UNDER ATTACK

The original French version began with a Frankish knight travelling on the well-worn pilgrim path to the shrine of St James at Santiago de Compostela in northwest Spain. In his company was his daughter, recently widowed, and pregnant by her dead husband. The Frankish knight was killed in an attack by Fenix, King of Muslim Spain, and the daughter was taken into captivity. At Fenix's court – supposedly at Naples – the daughter gave birth, on Palm Sunday, to a girl, Blanchefleur, while on the same day Fenix's wife gave birth to a son, Floris.

The two children were raised together and when the time was ripe they fell in love. Fenix, wanting to prevent his son from marrying a Christian, sent Lady Blanchefleur away to Cairo (called Babylon in the poem), telling his son that his love

◄ *Cherubs look joyfully on as Tancred baptizes the Muslim maiden, Clorinda, in the climax of* Jerusalem Delivered.

▲ *For veteran crusaders and pilgrims, stories of Christianity and Islam at odds in love were an intriguing recasting of the war of the faiths fought out in the Holy Land.*

was dead. Sir Floris's grief was so extravagant that King Fenix, fearing his son might die, told him the truth. Sir Floris immediately travelled to Cairo to find her.

He found her incarcerated in a 'tower of maidens' kept for the pleasure of the emir, or ruler, of Cairo. Each year the emir selected a new virgin from the tower to be his wife, and killed the previous one. Floris played chess against the tower watchman, and managed to get himself smuggled into the tower by hiding inside a basket of flowers. There he encountered Lady Blanchefleur, and the couple were blissfully reunited. However, the emir grew suspicious and, visiting the tower, he caught Floris and Lady Blanchefleur together. His impulse was to kill them, but he restrained himself and asked his advisers, who were impressed by the intense love that the couple had for each other and asked that he spare them.

Floris was knighted by the emir, upon which he married Lady Blanchefleur; meanwhile, Blanchefleur's friend Lady Claris married the emir, who repented of the wickedness he had formerly shown and promised to kill no more brides. Shortly afterwards, the news arrived that

Sir Floris's father King Fenix had died, and Floris and Lady Blanchefleur therefore returned to Spain. Sir Floris converted to Christianity and ruled justly with his Christian bride. He even persuaded the people of his kingdom to convert to Christianity as well.

The English version of the story emphasized the chastity of the lovers. When discovered by the emir they told him that they had not consummated their love and he tested their claim by making Lady Blanchefleur bathe her hands in magical water that would discolour if she were not a virgin. She passed the test and as a result, in honour of their chaste self-control, the emir set them both free.

AUCASSIN AND NICOLETTE

Another popular tale of love across the religious divide was that of *Aucassin et Nicolette*, an early-13th-century French *chantefable* (a story intended for singing at court, proceeding through alternating segments of sung verses and recited sections of prose). It told of the love between Aucassin (a Christian knight and the son of the count of Beaucaire) and a Saracen maiden in captivity, Nicolette. It is thought to have been based on the same Greco-Byzantine original as *Floire et Blancheflor*.

Nicolette, daughter of the king of Carthage, was stolen as a young girl by slave traders and ended up as a servant of Sir Garin, Count of Beaucaire, near Arles in Provence. Sir Garin's son Sir Aucassin saw the slave girl and began to fantasize about her. He had been a very promising knight, a strong young man of great prowess, but now he began to abandon the military arts of war and just drifted about, dreaming of Nicolette.

The situation became so bad that when the town was besieged, Sir Aucassin refused to help his father in the fight, declaring that he wanted only to ponder on his love for Nicolette. Then his father was furious and sent Nicolette away, although he did not tell Sir Aucassin. Eventually Sir Aucassin said he would fight for the defence of his city if he could

▲ *The forest, the place where Aucassin and Nicolette (and other lovers of romance) were reunited, is presented as a place untouched by the laws of the world.*

see Nicolette one more time. His father agreed, without admitting that he had sent her away, and Sir Aucassin spearheaded the garrison of the town to a great victory over the besieging army.

Then Sir Garin admitted what he had done to Nicolette. Sir Aucassin was overcome with distress. He went for a ride in the magical forest nearby, and discovered Nicolette there. They were together for a while, but later travelled to a distant land, and became separated again. Nicolette returned to her father in Carthage and Aucassin travelled sadly home.

The final stage of the drama began when Nicolette set forth from her home disguised as a minstrel, with her face darkened by berry juice, determined to track her lord down. She came to France and performed a song before Sir Aucassin, who did not recognize her. The song, about a lady called Nicolette, moved Sir Aucassin to tears, and he offered the minstrel a vast amount of money to travel to Carthage in order to persuade the lady to return. Then, seeing that her beloved lord was still deeply devoted to her, Lady Nicolette revealed her true identity and the lovers were joyfully reunited.

INTO THE OTHERWORLD
KNIGHTS AND THEIR FAIRY LOVERS

It was a common theme in courtly romances for knights to enter into a mysterious 'Otherworld', where they could became lovers of fairy noblewomen. They could generally come and go from this Otherworld without harm, although there was often an element of danger attached to their dealings with ladies and lords of that often menacing world.

LANVAL AND HIS LADY

In the intriguing 12th-century lay, or narrative song, *Lanval*, a knight of King Arthur had been reduced to poverty because the king was failing to support him, but he found a lover and a patroness in the fairy world. The poem was one of 12 Anglo-Norman lays written by a woman poet known to history as Marie de France (see box). The poems explored and glorified the themes of courtly love.

The song of *Lanval* described how one day Sir Lanval was wandering in the meadow near King Arthur's court when he was waylaid by two lovely fairy maidens – one was carrying water in a golden bowl, while the other held a towel. They took him to the fabulously wealthy home of their beautiful mistress. This Otherworld home was an elegant pavilion, topped with a golden eagle, and was found nearby as if beyond an invisible barrier in the meadow. The lady became Sir Lanval's lover and said she would appear

> ### MARIE DE FRANCE
> The author of the lay *Lanval* is known as Marie de France on the basis of a line in the epilogue to a collection of fables she wrote. Marie, whose poems were known in the 12th century, is the oldest known woman poet in French literature. Her delightful and very well-composed songs were almost certainly an influence on the work of later trouvères. Marie may have been Marie de Champagne, daughter of Eleanor of Aquitaine, but since there is some evidence that her poems were written in England, it is more likely that she was Marie, the Abbess of Shaftesbury, half-sister of King Henry II of England, or Marie the Countess of Boulogne, daughter of King Stephen of England, or Marie de Meulan, daughter of a great French lord, who was married to Hugh Talbot. She dedicated the lays to 'a noble king', thought to be Henry II or his son, Henry the Young King.

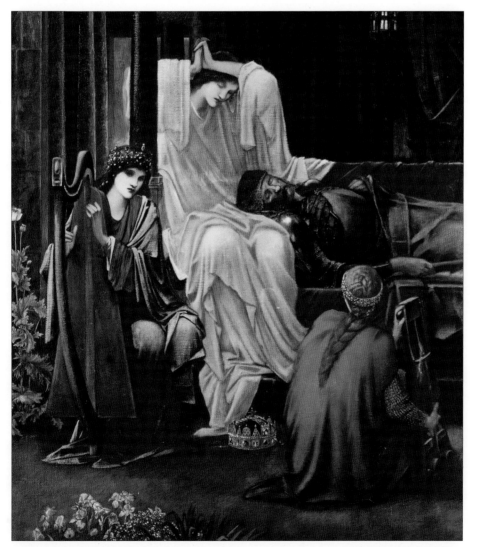

to him whenever he wished and make him as rich as he could want on one condition: that he must not tell another person of her existence. If he did, she would abandon him forever.

Sir Lanval happily accepted her terms. He enjoyed the comfort of eating and dressing well, and of being able to exhibit the chivalric virtue of *largesse* at court. He became known for his generosity: he would ransom prisoners, pay for jugglers and *jongleurs* and feed those without a patron of their own. His lady was happy

◄ *The Isle of Avalon, where Arthur is said to lie asleep, ready to come to the aid of England in her hour of greatest need, is part of the Otherworld realm. Ladies of that land attend him in his deathly sleep.*

for him to do as he pleased, as long as he did not break the one condition of their relationship – its secrecy.

However, one day Queen Guinevere approached Sir Lanval and attempted to seduce him. He rejected her advances, and she declared that he clearly did not like women. He retaliated rashly, declaring that he had a lady of his own who was fairer by far than Queen Guinevere.

Guinevere then accused Sir Lanval of trying to seduce her and denounced him for saying that a chambermaid was more beautiful than she was. Sir Lanval was called before the king in a full court with jury to answer for his actions. The jury declared that if Lanval could produce his mistress and prove that she was more beautiful than Guinevere he should go free. Lanval's heart sank as he realized that he had broken the terms of his agreement with his fairy mistress and that he could never expect her to help him again.

However, at the final moment the fairy mistress appeared before the court to prove that her knight had spoken the truth. She explained that even though he

▼ In 'La Belle Dame Sans Merci', English poet John Keats wrote of a beautiful fairy lady who captivated a knight-at-arms and robbed him of all his energy and purpose.

had broken their agreement, she did not want harm to come to him. All present, even King Arthur, were captivated by the beauty of this fairy lady, and they agreed that she was more beautiful even than Queen Guinevere.

As the lady was leaving, Sir Lanval leapt on the back of her white horse and rode away with her into the mists of magic. The poet said that Sir Lanval was never seen again, for she carried him off to the Isle of Avalon, the fabled final resting place of King Arthur himself.

Encounters with fairy women and the Otherworld were common in the Celtic folklore that fed into both the Arthurian romance tradition and into the Breton lays. The story of Sir Lanval, for example, may have had a common folkloric source with the story of Sir Yvain (as described in Chrétien de Troyes's *Yvain, the Knight of the Lion*), for Yvain also met a lady associated with water, and broke a promise to her.

SIR GUINGAMOR

Another Breton lay told the story of Sir Guingamor, with many similar themes to that of Sir Lanval (it was once thought to be another work of Marie de France, but modern historians think this unlikely). In

▲ Knights who had encounters with ladies of the fairy realm risked losing control of their destiny. Here King Arthur himself lies in a daze before the queen of the fairies.

this story, the knight was approached by the Queen of Brittany, who tried to seduce him, but he resisted her advances and so she taunted him, daring him to go on the hunt for the white boar – a task that had already cost the lives of ten knights. Like any good knight, Sir Guingamor could not resist the challenge to his prowess and his reputation, and departed on the quest with the king's horse and dogs.

While on the hunt he found a green marble palace and beyond it a beautiful maiden bathing in a pool. She promised him help if he stayed as her lover for three days; he did so and afterwards was able to catch the boar. His fairy lover allowed him to return to his home but warned him that he could not eat anything while there. When he returned to Brittany he found that three centuries had passed. Forgetting his instruction not to eat, he bit into a wild apple, and immediately became extremely weak. He was led back to the Otherworld and installed in the green marble palace by two beautiful maidens.

BRAVE KNIGHTS AND PHANTOM LADIES
LEGENDS OF MELUSINE AND THE HOUSE OF LUSIGNAN

A phantom lady, probably originally a water spirit from Celtic folklore, appeared repeatedly in the foundation myths of a number of noble and royal houses in medieval Europe. She was said to be the mother of crusader knight Guy de Lusignan, King Consort of Jerusalem.

The lady was half-woman, half-serpent, and could live among human society as long as she could keep her true nature secret. She therefore placed a prohibition on her noble lover ever seeing her bathe – in some versions of the tale, she revealed her true nature only on a Saturday or a Sunday, when she grew a scaly lower half. The most celebrated version of her tale was told by 15th-century French trouvère Jean d'Arras.

▼ *In a fateful moment, Count Raymond gives in to the temptation to spy on his fairy wife, and discovers her secret.*

▲ *It was believed that the fairy Melusine was a true ancestor of one of the most powerful families in medieval Europe, the family of de Lusignan. Here she is pictured as part of a genealogical family tree.*

According to this version, a Scottish king named Alynas met a beautiful lady named Pressyne in the forest when he was out hunting. He was captivated by her beauty and begged her to marry him, and she agreed on condition that he would not try to look at her when she was bathing. They lived together for some time, and Lady Pressyne gave birth to three girls, Melusine, Melior and Palatyne – but when King Alynas broke his promise not to spy on her, she left and fled to the Isle of Avalon with her daughters.

Melusine was later told of her father's actions, and she tried to punish him by locking him inside a mountain. For this she was herself punished, by being cursed to be a serpent from the waist down one day every week.

Years later Raymond de Lusignan was tracking a boar in the magical forests of France with his father. He had a chance to

▲ *Melusine escapes Raymond in the shape of a dragon, but returns secretly during the night to nurse her children.*

kill the beast, but his sword deflected off the creature's thick hide and killed the old man. In a panic Raymond fled through the forest until he came to a musical bubbling stream, beside which he met the three beautiful daughters of Lady Pressyne. He asked Melusine to marry him and she agreed, promising she would create a wonderful castle beside the forest stream for them to live in. Her only condition was that he should not try to see her on a Saturday, but on that one day a week he should leave her to her private ablutions.

Lady Melusine was as good as her word. She magically created a great fortress and lived there with Raymond for many years. Her 11 sons, including Guy de Lusignan, were all strong and skilled in the arts of war, and they brought great fame on their father's house through their exploits fighting for the cross on crusade. But all, like their mother, had a secret flaw.

One day, stung by gossip in the town, Raymond broke his promise not to spy on Melusine on a Saturday. He looked through the keyhole to see her bathing and discovered that she had a serpent's tail. He was shocked but decided to keep

the matter secret – however, one day they quarrelled over a sin committed by one of their sons and Raymond forgot his good sense and denounced his wife as a serpent. That day she changed into a dragon and left, deserting her two youngest children.

Lady Melusine never returned during the day. Her ghostly form could afterwards be seen at night suckling the two infants she had abandoned, but in the morning she would be gone. She was also said to materialize at the Lusignan castle when a count of the family was about to die.

Lady Melusine was also claimed as an ancestor by Holy Roman Emperor Henry VII and also by the royal house of Luxembourg. A similar fairy lady was proposed, as we have seen, as the ancestor of King Richard I of England in the romance of his life. Like many other fairy ladies she could not remain in the church when the Mass was being said, and fled when the Host (the Body of Christ) was raised up.

PARTONOPE AND MELIOR
A later 12th-century romance version of the tradition told how a French knight named Sir Partonope won back the hand of Melusine's sister, Lady Melior, through his prowess in the lists. The story had a traditional beginning – Sir Partonope was caught up by fairy magic while out on a

hunt for a boar and was transported to a magical castle where he was seduced in darkness by Lady Melior, whom he was not permitted to see.

Sir Partonope begged this phantom lady to be his wife and she agreed on condition that he would never try to look on her. After spending a full year with her in the fairy Otherworld, Sir Partonope had to return to France to help fight against an invasion by the Vikings, and afterwards he was tricked by his mother into marrying an earthly woman.

Later Sir Partonope came to his senses, rejected this new woman and tried to return to Lady Melior. His mother persuaded him to take a lantern in order to get at least a glimpse of his phantom love. When the light from the lantern fell on Lady Melior, he was banished and returned to France.

There he wandered, distraught, until deep in the forests he met Lady Melior's sister (here called Lady Urrake), who announced that a grand tournament was to be held nearby and that the knight who broke the most spears in the lists would have the honour of winning the hand of Lady Melior. She helped him and in the lists he proved his worth, winning the tournament and the most precious prize: his fairy wife's love.

THE IDEAL CHRISTIAN KNIGHT

ST GEORGE

St George was venerated as an exemplar of Christian chivalry in the Middle Ages. His image as the perfect holy warrior partly had its origins in the celebration of his deeds by the Eastern Orthodox Church, where he was shown as a soldier in iconography from the 7th century onwards. Crusaders would have seen and been influenced by this iconography.

George was a Christian martyr of the 3rd century, who was traditionally said to have met his end in Lydda (now Lod in Israel). We know nothing for sure about his life, but his story was developed by the 6th century and was known in western Europe by at least the 8th century. The knights who returned from the First Crusade greatly popularized his name and his chivalrous deeds.

MARTYRED BY DIOCLETIAN

According to his hagiography, he was the son of an officer in the Roman army from Cappadocia (an ancient region now part of Turkey) and a mother from Lydda, who

▼ *When George refused to persecute Christians, and declared his own faith in Christ, the Roman authorities executed him before the walls of Nicodemia.*

were both Christians. George was a superb soldier and rose through the ranks to become a member of the personal bodyguard of Emperor Diocletian.

In 303, according to the story, the emperor ordered a wave of persecution of Christians, but George revealed himself to be a Christian and refused to take part. He was savagely tortured. One of his terrible punishments was being tied to a wheel of swords. Finally he was beheaded at Nicodemia on 23 April 303. So nobly did he die, dedicating his soul to Christ, that his example convinced the Empress Alexandra and a pagan priest named Athanasius to turn to Christianity, for which they too were executed – in one account more than 1,000 Roman soldiers also converted and were put to death. George's body was taken to his mother's birthplace, Lydda, for burial.

A church built there during the reign of the first Christian emperor, Constantine I, was supposedly dedicated to George and housed his remains. It became a significant pilgrimage site. This building was destroyed in 1010, then the crusaders rebuilt it and dedicated it to St George. During the Third Crusade the army of the great Islamic general Saladin destroyed the holy building once more. It was finally rebuilt a second time in the 19th century.

GEORGE AND THE DRAGON

The celebrated story of St George and the dragon was originally told in the East, and was brought back to the West with the returning crusaders. In Europe it was recast within the conventions of medieval chivalric life – George was represented on a white charger, and killing the dragon with a lance like any knight at a tournament or in a crusader battle charge. The story was part of the very popular *Legenda Sanctorum* (*Saints' Readings*) – better known as *Legenda Aurea* (*Golden Legend*) – a collection of saints' lives written in *c.*1260 by Jacobus de Voragine, the arch-bishop of Genoa, which ensured its widespread dissemination.

The story told that the citizens of 'Silene' (perhaps Cyrene in Libya) or, in some sources, of George's hometown Lydda, were terrorized by a dragon that had taken up residence at the spring (or lake) where they drew their water. In order to get water, they had to entice the dragon away from the spring by offering animals and a young virgin, chosen by lots from the townspeople.

One day the victim chosen by chance was the princess, and although the king offered all his wealth in return for his daughter's life, the people refused to draw the lots again. She was sent out to the dragon but George arrived on his charger just as she was about to be given up to the beast. The princess tried to send him away, but George remained and made the sign of the cross before himself, as any good Christian warrior would before combat.

▼ *George's cult was strong in the Eastern Orthodox Church. An artist of the Novgorod School painted this icon in c.1150.*

▲ *George represents the Church and all the knights who support it as he rescues innocence in the form of the princess. This fresco of c.1350 is from Verona, Italy.*

Then George charged at the dragon with couched lance and wounded the beast severely. He called for the princess to throw him her girdle and he put this around the dragon's neck. The dragon came meekly along behind them to the town, where the people, upon seeing it, were very frightened; but George killed it as they watched. The citizens were so grateful to their saviour that they turned their backs on the pagan faith and converted to Christianity. In all the medieval romance accounts, St George's lance was called Ascalon after the city of Ashkelon (now in Israel), which was the scene of the concluding triumphant conflict of the First Crusade, when – fresh from their capture of Jerusalem – the crusaders defeated a relief army that had been sent by Fatimids of Egypt, in the Battle of Ascalon on 12 August 1099.

The dragon-slaying story is ancient and may have had its origin among the Indo-European tribes who spread out from the central Asian steppes to places as diverse as India, Greece and western Europe. It is found in myths from the ancient Near East (told by the Hittites), ancient India and ancient Greece.

PATRON SAINT

By the 14th century, St George was effectively the patron saint of knighthood. In 1348 King Edward III of England designated St George as the patron of his new knightly brotherhood, the Order of the Garter, and during Edward's reign George became recognized as the patron saint of England, replacing St Edmund in the role. During the reign of King Henry V of England (1413–22), St George's Day (23 April) was celebrated as a national holiday. George is also the patron of a very wide range of other countries including Greece, Montenegro, Georgia, Russia and Palestine, and of cities including Beirut and Moscow.

PATRON SAINTS AT WAR

SAINTS AS CHIVALRIC WARRIORS

◀ St James the Greater (far left) is the patron saint of Spain. Here he is shown with St Jude and St Simon the Zealot. All three were among Christ's twelve apostles.

At the Battle of Antioch in June 1098 the crusaders reported that they saw St George, St Demetrius and St Maurice fighting alongside them. (St Demetrius and St Maurice were, like George, both martyrs killed during the persecution of Christians in the Roman Empire.) The conflict at Antioch came at a time of heightened religious perceptions. Just before the clash, a monk named Peter Bartholomew claimed to have had a vision of St Andrew, reporting that the Holy Lance used to pierce Christ's side on the Cross was buried in Antioch, and after a search, the Lance was supposedly found. St Andrew then appeared once more and urged the crusaders to fast for five days in order to ensure victory.

The Battle of Antioch was quickly won and the saints, particularly St George,

became associated with the success of the First Crusade. While fighting in Palestine during the Third Crusade of 1189–92 King Richard I of England put the English army under the protection of St George. About the same time, the banner of St George (the red cross on a white background) became the accepted garb for English soldiers.

ST ANDREW AND SCOTTISH TRADITIONS

St Andrew had become established as the patron saint of Scotland in around the 10th century. In the Bible, Andrew was a fisherman on the Sea of Galilee and the brother of Simon Peter, the first pope; he was martyred on a diagonally shaped cross (of the kind shown on the flag of Scotland; known as a saltire in heraldry) at his own

request, because he declared himself unworthy to be crucified on a cross that was identical to the kind used to kill his Lord. According to Scottish legend, St Andrew's relics had been brought with God's guidance from Constantinople to the town of St Andrews in Scotland. A story told that a Pictish king named Ongus (probably Oengus mac Fergus of the Picts, 729–761) had seen a cloud in the shape of St Andrew's cross when fighting the English, and declared that the saint was overseeing the battle and leading the Scottish warriors on to victory.

LEGENDS OF ST GEORGE

There was a well-established tradition of legends and romance stories that presented the saints as chivalric warriors. The English prose romance *The Famous History of the Seven Champions of Christendom* (1596) celebrated the legendary achievements of the patron saints of England, Wales, Ireland, Scotland, Italy, France and

▼ Weak from hunger but strong in their faith, the crusaders defeated a large army at Antioch. They attributed the unlikely victory to the saints who fought with them.

Spain, St Anthony of Italy, St Andrew of Scotland, St Patrick of Ireland, and St David of Wales. St George turned against the lady and imprisoned her in rock. Then he set the saints free and they embarked upon a series of adventures.

St George himself travelled to Egypt, where he killed a silver-scaled dragon and so saved King Ptolemy's daughter Lady Sabra, who was its next intended victim. Lady Sabra fell in love with St George, which enraged her suitor, King Almidor of Morocco.

King Almidor plotted against St George and sent him to the sultan of Persia with a letter. Without realizing, George was carrying his own death warrant, for the letter said he should be put to death as an enemy of Islam. He was thrown in jail, but on the day of his execution overawed his captor in the style of Richard I: two lions were sent into his cell and he plunged his hands into the animals' chests and tore their hearts out. He was spared execution, but imprisoned for seven years.

▼ *According to one tradition, St George went on to marry the princess he had saved from the dragon.*

UNDONE BY SORCERY

Finally George escaped and was reunited with the other seven patron saints. He sent the other six saints to Persia to defeat the sultan and his Saracen army. They did so in a five-day battle, but then they all fell victim to the tricks of a sorcerer who summoned up a glittering pavilion and a harem of beautiful maidens to entice the saints. The six champions, although saints, fell victim to this temptation and followed the maidens into the pavilion.

At this point St George arrived and he alone of all the saints was able to see through the sorcerer's spell. He pulled down the pavilion and set the other six champions free from enchantment for a second time. A final battle against the pagan forces of Persia followed, which ended in the death of 200,000 enemies of the Christian faith.

St George then enacted the pattern of the Crusades: a religious war led to political gains. He became ruler of Persia and parcelled out the lands he had gained among the other patron saints. Afterwards, all seven patron saints marched home to Europe. They made many converts to Christianity on their journey back.

▲ *St Andrew, patron saint of Scotland, had many martial associations. According to St John's Gospel, St Andrew was originally a disciple of John the Baptist.*

Spain. It was written towards the close of the age of chivalry by English romance author Richard Johnson, who drew on a centuries-old popular tradition of tales about saints fighting as brave knights against great armies full of heathens and riding to the rescue of courtly maidens.

Johnson's romance claimed that St George was the son of the High Steward of England and was born after his mother dreamed that she was about to give birth to a dragon. He came into the world with a red cross on his hand and an image of a dragon on his chest.

Like many a knight of romance before him, he was raised by a fairy lady in the wilderness of the woods. When George came of age, the lady presented him with his chivalric equipment: a suit of armour made of steel from Libya that reflected the light of heaven, a horse named Bayard (like that of the Carolingian hero Renaud of Montauban) and a sword named Ascalon, supposedly made by the ancient Greek Cyclops.

The lady then showed George an enchanted castle in the forest where she had imprisoned the other patron saints of Europe: St Denis of France, St James of

OUTLAW KNIGHTS

HEREWARD THE WAKE AND EDRIC OF SHREWSBURY

Alongside stories about the chivalric achievements of saints and biblical warriors, of the paladins of Charlemagne, of King Arthur's followers and of crusader knights, there was a medieval tradition of romance tales about outlaw knights. In England this tradition had its roots in popular narratives about Saxon and British warriors who fought the Norman invasion in the 11th century.

Prominent among these Saxon and British opponents of the Normans were Hereward and Edric. Hereward was a nobleman from Lincolnshire who led resistance to King William I of England from a base at Ely, deep in the treacherous fens, but finally succumbed to the power of the Norman war machine. He was the subject of a vigorous popular tradition, notably celebrated in the 15th-century *Gesta Herewardi* (*Deeds of Hereward*) by 'Ingulph of Crowland', Benedictine abbot at Croyland Abbey, Lincolnshire.

LINCOLNSHIRE LANDOWNER

Hereward appeared in the historical record as a landowner in Lincolnshire listed in the Domesday Survey. The *Anglo-Saxon Chronicle* named him as the leader of an

▼ *The Hereward tradition celebrated fierce native resistance to the Normans. His byname is believed to mean 'the Watchful'.*

▲ *Some accounts claim that Hereward was the son of Leofric, Earl of Mercia, and his wife Godiva, who famously rode naked in the streets of Coventry to persuade her husband to lift a toll imposed on his tenants.*

assault in 1070 on Peterborough Abbey, launched to protest the appointment of a Norman abbot named Turold. Afterwards, the *Chronicle* states, he retreated to Ely, and withstood Norman attacks for a year, then escaped when the rebel stronghold fell.

COURTLY ADVENTURES

The legends cast Hereward as a figure from courtly romance. They told that he was a wild character, who caused so much trouble to his noble father that he was banished from his estate. He then went on a series of romance adventures: tracking and killing a bear in Scotland; rescuing a lady from a giant in Cornwall; fighting in Ireland; then being shipwrecked in Flanders, where after a brief imprisonment he met his wife, Lady Tulfrida, and found a marvellous horse named Swallow.

A KNIGHT IN FLANDERS

It is likely that these adventures had some historical foundation: Hereward appears to have rebelled against King Edward the Confessor, unhappy at the monarch's close connections with the Normans, and was banished from England. In exile he found employment as a mercenary knight in the service of Baldwin V, Count of Flanders. He would have learned chivalry during this sojourn in Flanders.

According to the legend, Hereward returned to England in 1068 only to discover that his father's lands had been seized by the Normans, who had also killed his younger brother and stuck the dead man's decapitated head above the gateway to the family home. In that moment, Hereward dedicated his life to fighting the Normans. He killed the men responsible for his brother's death and gathered rebels around him at Ely. There on an island amid the marshes of fenland, they were besieged by the might of the Norman army, which was led by King William himself.

▶ *William defeats the Anglo-Saxon King Harold, and Norman rule begins in England, in this illumination, c.1280–1300.*

ASSAULT ON ELY

The Normans first tried to attack head-on, building a wooden causeway for their troops across the marshlands. But the causeway collapsed into the mud and many knights lost their lives and valuable equipment in the marshland. Then the Normans tried to bring the rebels down with magic: William employed a witch, who promised to cast a spell that would disarm the Saxons.

Hereward was determined to find out what the Normans were planning, and visited the besiegers' camp disguised as a wandering potter. There he heard the witch discussing her plans. He was not well disguised, however, and was almost discovered, and after getting into a fight in the kitchens he escaped. Just before he disappeared back into the safety of the fenland, he humiliated one of the finest Norman knights by disarming him and

THE WILD HUNT

Both Hereward and Edric were said to ride in the Wild Hunt, a stampede of hunters, horses and dogs thought to be fairies or spirits of the dead, which was seen hurtling through the forests or sometimes the sky. Seeing the Wild Hunt was said to presage a disaster. In various traditions across Europe, the great figures of chivalry were said to be seen riding at the head of the Hunt: they included Charlemagne, with Roland carrying his standard; King Arthur; and Dietrich of Berne, the Germanic hero-king based on the 6th-century King Thedoric the Great of the Ostrogoths. Another leader of the Hunt was 'Herne the Hunter' who, according to the legend, was a huntsman in Windsor Park who had saved King Richard II's life then went mad and killed himself.

sending him back to his companions with the news that they had missed the opportunity to capture Hereward himself.

Hereward and the rebels set a fire in the marshland that foiled the Normans' next attack. The blaze scattered the besiegers in all directions and the witch broke her neck in the ensuing panic. Eventually the Normans succeeded in reaching their island after the monks of the abbey of Ely showed the attackers a safe way across the marshes, but Hereward and his men, forewarned, took to their boats and vanished into the mists.

One version of the legend suggested that because of his great skill as a warrior Hereward was pardoned by William, and his lands were restored, but another suggested that he was finally tracked down and killed by the Normans.

WILD EDRIC

Another staunch opposer of William I was celebrated in legend as 'Wild Edric'. Edric was a Mercian aristocrat, believed to have been Earl of Shrewsbury, known by a

Latin name, Edric Sylvaticus ('Edric of the Woods') – because he primarily waged guerrilla warfare from the wilderness of the forests. Edric fought the Normans on the English–Welsh borders in *c.*1067–70. The *Anglo-Saxon Chronicle* reported that with a group of Welsh allies he attacked the Norman garrison at Hereford in 1067. He was also said to have been defeated by King William at Shrewsbury in 1069. In common with many of the local thegns, he had his land seized by force and then simply given to Norman lords; it was handed to either Ranulph de Mortimer or William FitzOsbern.

In the tales of Wild Edric he was said to have become lost while out hunting in the forests and to have taken a fairy bride. Like many other knights, he was deprived of his Otherworldly lady by failing to keep to an agreement – in this case not to speak of her origins. In Shropshire, Edric was celebrated as a warrior-leader in time of need, said to live in local lead-mines and be ready to ride forth at some future date when his country needed him sorely.

THE SCOURGE OF THE VIKINGS

SIR GUY OF WARWICK

Hero of English and French romances from the 13th to the 17th centuries, the legendary Guy of Warwick was celebrated as a native English opponent of Viking invaders, a knight errant, a vanquisher of fantastic monsters and paragon of Christian chivalry who rode to the Holy Land and defeated countless Saracens before finally retiring as a religious hermit. His story, probably written for the Norman earls of Warwick, is a good example of the 'ancestral romances' that were produced to glorify the origins of noble houses in the Middle Ages.

The oldest version of Sir Guy's story was probably in a 12th-century French tale. It was then reworked in English and Anglo-Norman versions. The oldest surviving manuscript is the 13th-century Anglo-Norman work *Gui de Warewic*; the oldest English version dates to *c.*1300. The central event in Guy's legend was the defeat in single combat of a mighty Danish warrior named Colbrand, a victory that was said to have saved King Athelstan of England when his capital Winchester was besieged by a Viking army led by kings Anlaf and Gonelaph. This may have had a historical foundation in the invasion of

▼ *The popularity of the Guy of Warwick tales derives in large part from their hero's successes in fighting Danish invaders.*

southern England by Danish troops in 993, although Winchester was actually saved from capture following payment of a bribe rather than victory by any English champion in single combat.

PARAGON OF CHIVALRY

The versions of Guy of Warwick's romance that survive probably contain additions by monastic scribes, for they include a wealth of religious elements. The legend of Guy remained extremely popular for centuries. In the 16th century his reputation as a great Christian knight was so high that he was included in contemporary lists of the 'Nine Worthies'.

According to the legend of his life, Guy was the son of the steward in the service of the earl of Warwick, and he was in love with the earl's daughter, Lady Felice. He was raised to knighthood, and to prove himself worthy of her love embarked on a career of knight errantry. He fought in numerous tournaments in France and Germany; then he freed the daughter of the emperor of Germany after she had been kidnapped; killed a dragon; he then went to Constantinople and fought against great armies of Saracens. He defeated the Saracens' champion Coldran in single combat, then killed the king of Tyre and the sultan of Constantinople. On his return to Warwick he was greeted as a

▲ *King Athelstan kneels before the warrior-turned-mendicant Guy. Athelstan was the first king to rule all of England.*

great Christian knight, a humbler of the enemies of the Christian faith, and Lady Felice finally agreed to become his wife.

PENITENT KNIGHT

However, almost immediately after the wedding, Sir Guy had a vision of Christ, who told him to undertake a penitential journey. Therefore Sir Guy embarked on a pilgrimage to the Holy Land. Perhaps mindful of the fate of Lady Laudine, wife of the Arthurian knight Sir Yvain, who was forgotten by her knight while he was away on a journey of knight errantry, Lady Felice gave Sir Guy a ring to wear, saying that each time he looked on it he should remember her. He wore the ring during his pilgrimage, on which he had many more extraordinary adventures, including conflicts with great giants.

Returning to Warwick once more, he defeated the Dun Cow, a vast cow that was terrorizing the countryside, as well as a boar in Windsor Park and a serpent in Northumberland. After these exploits, he

▲ *The lords and earls of Warwick are commemorated in this chronicle roll, written c.1477–85 by John Rous, priest at the chapel established at Guy's Cliffe.*

fought the Danish champion, Colbrand, who was holding Winchester under siege. The events were said to have taken place in 9th-century England, during the reign of King Athelstan. According to local Winchester tradition the battle against Colbrand took place by the walls of the Benedictine Abbey of Hyde, just outside

THE ANCESTRAL ROMANCE

Sir Guy's legends are examples of the 'ancestral romance': stories that celebrate the establishment of a noble house, or a branch of a family – in this case the earls of Warwick. These poems turn into legendary form the family's past elevation to greatness – as in this legend through the rise by way of martial exploits from humble origins to being fit to enter the established nobility as an equal of Lady Felice. Another of this type of ancestral romance is the Lusignan legend that built family history on the folklore about the water-spirit Melusine.

the city walls. (Hyde Abbey was demolished by Henry VIII in the mid-16th century Dissolution of the Monasteries.)

LIFE AS A HERMIT

Guy's victory over Colbrand won him King Athelstan's devotion. Afterwards, the knight returned to Warwick, but in disguise in order to hide himself away in a hermitage, to spend his last days in prayer and penitence after a life of violence in which he had spilled a great deal of blood. Each day he attended the house of his wife, Lady Felice, disguised in rags, in order to beg for alms. Finally as the appointed day of his death drew near, and he came to know for certain that he was to be called from his life on earth, he sent Lady Felice the ring so that at last she knew what had happened to her husband. She joined him at his hermitage and they were united for the last few days of Sir Guy's life.

GUY'S CLIFFE

The memory of Sir Guy was proudly celebrated in Warwick. Local legend claimed to have established the scene of his later hermitage to be a cliff in rocks above the River Avon just outside the town – a place afterwards called Guy's Cliffe. In 1394 a tower was added to Warwick Castle and

named in his honour, and supposed relics of his life, including his sword and pot, were collected there. A chantry (chapel) was established at Guy's Cliffe, complete with a statue of Guy, in 1423 by Richard de Beauchamp, 13th Earl of Warwick. A country house was built on the site in the 18th century, but it is now a ruin.

▼ *Christ commanded Guy to make penance for his many acts of violence by travelling to the Holy Land. This image is from the Athelstan Psalter (c.950) from Winchester.*

ROBBER KNIGHTS

EUSTACE THE MONK AND ROBERT LE DIABLE

◄ *The tale of Norman knight Robert the Devil – perhaps based on the life of Duke Robert II of Normandy – was popular in later centuries. This scene is from an 1831 opera about Robert by Giacomo Meyerbeer.*

Some knights of legend and romance were celebrated as anti-heroes for their wicked deeds pursued with great energy. One such story was that of Eustace the Monk, which told of an outlaw knight who was versed in black magic, switched sides at his convenience and accumulated a fortune as a naval mercenary. Similar tales were told in the legend of Robert the Devil, but in his case the wickedness had a purpose, for it led him eventually to take heed of his conscience and he ended his life a glowing example of Christian penitence and religious chivalry.

EUSTACE THE MONK

The romance of Eustace the Monk was written in the mid-13th century by a poet from Picardy. It was based on the exploits of a nobleman's son from Boulogne. According to the historical record, this Eustace was the seneschal of Renaud de Dammartin, Count of Boulogne, but in around 1204 Eustace was accused of being dishonest, declared an outlaw and had his lands confiscated.

He fled into the deep forest, then became a naval mercenary in the English Channel. He worked for King John of England in 1205–12, commanding a fleet of 30 ships and leading raids along the Normandy coast. With the king's backing he seized the Channel Island of Sark as his base. In 1212, however, he switched sides and began to raid English ports. In 1215 he supported the revolt by rebel barons against King John's rule and he lost his life in 1217 when, while carrying supplies by sea to the rebels in England, he was intercepted by an English fleet and decapitated.

The romance of Eustace followed the facts of this life story quite closely, adding that early in life Eustace had travelled to Toledo in Spain and studied black magic while he was there. It also stated that he became a Benedictine monk in France before embarking on his life of crime and mercenary exploits, and he only left the religious life in order to avenge the death of his father.

The romance told a number of stories in which Eustace put his powers of black magic to the service of his pleasure or in order to enact his revenge. One such tale recounts the time when, after an abbot of a monastery refused to feed him, Eustace brought a pig's carcass to life in the shape of a hideous old woman and made her fly around the refectory driving the monks mad with fear and leaving the way clear for Eustace to seat himself at the high table and enjoy the food on offer.

▼ *The romance of the wicked knight Robert the Devil was still very popular in the 16th century. This is the title page to* The Terrible and Marvellous Life of Robert the Devil, *published in 1563.*

THE WICKEDNESS OF ROBERT THE DEVIL

The legend of Robert the Devil told the story of a French knight, the son of the Devil, cursed to only use his strength in battle for immoral ends. He sought forgiveness and found salvation by riding out as an unknown knight to save Europe three times from Saracen attack. His name and story were connected to those of King William I of England's father Robert II, Duke of Normandy, also known as 'Robert the Devil'.

Duke Robert II of Normandy won a reputation for wickedness, and the nickname 'the Devil', by poisoning his own elder brother Richard in order to win power for himself in Normandy. Both Robert's children – William and Adelaide of Normandy – were illegitimate; they were the offspring of Robert's mistress, Herleva of Falaise.

Towards the end of his life, Robert made William his heir in Normandy and departed on pilgrimage to the Holy Land. According to the account in the *Gesta Normanorum Ducum* (*Deeds of the Norman Dukes*), written by a monk named William of Jumièges in *c*.1060, Robert succeeded in reaching Jerusalem but died on the return journey at Nicaea (modern Iznik, Turkey) in July 1035.

The oldest known version of the legend of Robert the Devil was written in Latin by a Dominican friar named Stephen of Bourbon in *c*.1250. It was rewritten as a 13th-century French metrical romance and was also the subject of a 14th-century miracle play. In the late 15th century, it achieved great popularity as a printed romance, first in French and later in English and Spanish.

THE DEVIL'S CHILD

According to the legend, Robert's mother was unable to have a child and turned to the Devil to help her become pregnant. From his earliest youth Robert was a chivalric prodigy, superb in the saddle, unbeatable in the lists, feared by knights who saw him at large in the countryside.

But because of his father, he was incapable of putting his strength to good use. He was so troubled by his wickedness that he went to the pope to ask for help, and the pope sent him to a hermit who possessed such extraordinary saintliness that he had won dominion even over the evil works of the devil. The hermit told Robert to put himself through a demanding series of penances designed to defeat his self-will. He had to take a vow of silence, get food from the mouth of a dog and endeavour to bring about situations in which he would be ridiculed and humiliated. Robert gladly did these things and at last found peace in his soul.

▼ *Nicaea, where Duke Robert II died, was an important city from classical times, and in 1097 was the scene of the first major action of the First Crusade.*

THE UNKNOWN KNIGHT

However, at this point the city of Rome came under threat from a great Saracen army and memories of Robert's fierceness in battle were still fresh enough to make men call upon him to come to the aid of the Christian city. At first he did not want to go back to life in the saddle, but an angel of God descended to convince him that it was necessary. He rode out as an unidentified knight, without heraldic device on his shield or helmet, and three times he single-handedly drove off the besieging Saracen army.

Finally Robert had succeeded in saving his soul. In variant endings of the legend he was either rewarded with the hand in marriage of the Holy Roman Emperor's fair daughter, or he retired to a hermitage, where he lived out his last days in peace and great holiness.

KNIGHTS OF THE FOREST

FULK FITZWARIN AND ROBIN HOOD

Some knights of legend and romance fought as outlaws because they had been wrongly dispossessed, and were only trying to regain their rightful inheritance. One such outlaw was the Shropshire knight turned forest raider Fulk Fitzwarin.

THE HISTORICAL FULK FITZWARINS

The deeds of Fulk Fitzwarin were celebrated in an English verse romance that is now lost but which was summarized in French, Latin and English versions that do survive. The romance accounts were based on the life of a landowner of that name who lost his property at Whittington, Shropshire, following a lawsuit in 1200. He then spent three years as an outlaw in the forests before being granted a royal pardon in 1203. Then he lived as a knight until 1215, when he joined the barons' revolt against King John. In this period he lost his property again, but regained it after John's death in 1216 and then he spent his remaining years on his estate until he died in the mid-1250s. This life history may combine those of two knights called Fulk Fitzwarin, father and son.

The romance described how Fulk had been raised at the royal court at Windsor Castle following the death of his father, and in this period had quarrelled violently with the future King John over a game of chess. John was losing, it was said, so he turned the board over, scattering the pieces, and hit Fulk in the mouth; Fulk simply hit him back, so John ran to his father King Henry to complain, but Henry told his son off for telling tales. John did not forget this childhood humiliation.

FOREST OUTLAW

In 1200 John got his revenge by dispossessing Fulk of his lands at Whittington and giving them to a rival lord. Fulk swore that he would not serve such a king and with his brothers took to the forests of

▲ *Far from the safety of court or castle, hunting with a few retainers, kings and great lords were vulnerable to attack. King John was ambushed by Fulk Fitzwarin.*

Shropshire. There he made his living by robbing King John's wagon trains and his soldiers. In true romance style, he next had an overseas adventure, spending a period as a pirate in the English Channel, rescuing the daughter of the king of Orkney and saving the duke of Carthage from a dragon.

On his return to England he and his brothers heard that King John was holding court at Windsor Castle and travelled to Windsor Forest. One day when King John rode out hunting, Fulk disguised himself as a charcoal burner and led the king into a trap, where his brothers and supporters were waiting. They surrounded the royal party and made the king promise to become Fulk Fitzwarin's friend once more. But John was dishonest, and as

soon as he had been released he sent Sir James de Normandy out with an armed force to capture Fulk.

IN SIR JAMES'S ARMOUR

In the forest, Fulk was warned that the knight and his men were coming, and he laid another trap. He captured Sir James and then exchanged suits of armour and horses with him. Fulk rode into the castle at Windsor, pretending to be Sir James, and presented the real Sir James to the king as 'the prisoner Fulk Fitzwarin'. Fulk got away with the trick and rode off on a fresh horse provided by King John, before the king had lifted the visor of the prisoner's helmet and discovered that his leading knight had been humiliated by the forest outlaw.

Subsequently there was another great battle in the forest during which Fulk was injured and his brother William was taken captive. Fulk escaped on a horse with the Earl of Chester, rode hard to the coast and managed to make his escape to Spain. He enjoyed further adventures, this time on the Barbary Coast of Africa, before he returned to England to free his brother from the Tower of London. Subsequently he captured King John once more while the king was out hunting, and finally he was able to force him to make peace. Fulk was no longer an outlaw and his castle and lands were restored to him.

ROBIN HOOD

Another great figure of English legend and folklore, Robin Hood, made his living as an outlaw in the forests and was often celebrated as a scourge of King John. In the earliest ballads Robin was just a humble yeoman, but from the 16th century, when his stories were printed, he was presented like Fulk Fitzwarin as a noble knight deprived of his rightful lands. Some versions of the tale also identified him as a crusader knight who returned from his service in the Holy Land to discover that

▲ *Emerging from the forest, Robin and other outlaws have the danger and force that were associated with the teeming natural world, outside the order of a town.*

▼ *One great figure of chivalry hosts another, as Robin Hood and his merry men entertain Richard Coeur de Lion in the forest. Robin lost some of his original menace when he was transformed in legend from an anarchic robber to a supporter of the crusader king.*

his lands had been seized by the corrupt officials of the usurping King John.

There was probably never a single historical figure on which the legends of Robin Hood are based, for the name first appeared in the 13th century as a general one for outlaws. By the following century, popular rhymes were celebrating the feats of a particular legendary outlaw of this name. The tradition of Robin Hood was based on the deeds of actual outlaws such as Hereward the Wake, Eustace the Monk and Fulk Fitzwarin.

In the 15th and 16th centuries Robin Hood was incorporated into May Day festivities, with people dressing as characters from the ballads, a practice that was popular at the court of King Henry VIII. In the early ballads the events were said to take place in the reign of King Edward (without specifying exactly which one), but in the 16th century the stories were relocated to the 1190s, when King John's corruption blighted the lives of the people of England.

INDEX

▲ *Lancelot and Guinevere.*

▲ *Tristan and Iseult.*

▲ *Sir Yvain and his lion.*

▼ *Sir Lancelot.*

▲ *Beaumaris Castle.*

▼ *Medieval heraldic devices.*

▲ *The quest for the grail.*

▼ *A castle besieged.*

▲ *A knight at prayer.*

▼ *The Battle of Crécy.*